TEXAS STATE PARKS BUCKET JOURNAL

Visit the State Parks and Historic Sites of Texas, USA

This book belongs to

____

If found please call

____

"**You may** all go to hell, and I will go to Texas".
~ Davy Crockett

"**Texas is** neither southern nor western. Texas is Texas"
~Senator William Blakley

"**Texas is** a state of mind. Texas is an obsession. Above all, Texas is a nation in every sense of the word."
~John Steinbeck

"**In Texas**, we practically come out of the womb in jeans."
~Kelly Clarkson

TEXAS STATE PARKS
BUCKET JOURNAL

ISBN:
Publisher: My Bucket Journals, LLC
PO Box 310, Hutto, Texas 78634

Disclaimer
The information in this book is based on the author's opinion, knowledge and experience. The publisher and the author will not be held liable for the use or misuse of the information contained herein.

Disclosure
This book may contain affiliate links. If you click through an affiliate link to a third-party website and make a purchase, the author may receive a small commission.

You are a proud Texan; a traveler, adventurer, and freedom lover who wants to experience your state and remember it.

In this Texas State Parks Bucket Journal, you will find pages for all 93 state parks, state natural areas, and state historic sites.

This bucket journal is different. It gives you the ability to create your own unique exploration of whichever state park or historic site you choose

How to Use Your Texas State Parks Bucket Journal

Search out details about the state park or historic site and plan the things you want to see on the left side of the 2-page spread.

This is best done before you take your trip, but can be done while you are out exploring.

On the right side, you will chronicle everything that you do and experience. Included is space for reflection about your stay in the park.

The Texas State Parks Bucket Journal will become a living memory for your trips and adventures as you discover the wonders of the state of Texas .

Enjoy exploring the beauty that is Texas!

TABLE OF CONTENTS

TABLE OF CONTENTS

Plan your trip with our interactive map.
Find it at
https://cutt.ly/texas-state-parks

GHOST TOWNS OF TEXAS

Ghost towns are primarily associated with the Wild West frontier and people flocking to areas with valuable mineral resources, including gold and silver in the Rockies and oil in Texas.

Just as it was important that the mines of Colorado and California could ship their riches out by rail, the vast cattle ranches of western plains needed to reach the rail head to turn their steers into cash. So the majority of ghost towns date from the 1880-1940 period of westward expansion and industrialization.

~Peter Ling, Professor of American Studies

15 Ghost Towns To Visit In Texas

1. Terlingua
2. Lobo
3. Glen Rio
4. Sherwood
5. Indianola
6. Barstow
7. The Grove
8. Independence
9. Medicine Mound
10. Belle Plain
11. Winkelmann
12. Clairemont
13. Catarina
14. Toyah
15. Gilliland

There are over 1000 abandoned towns in Texas!

Plan your Texas ghost town trip by visiting these websites

http://www.texasescapes.com/Texas-Ghost-Towns-A-to-Z.htm

https://en.wikipedia.org/wiki/List_of_ghost_towns_in_Texas

https://www.ghosttowns.com/states/tx/tx.html

Websites last checked 8/25/21

Abilene State Park

State: Texas　　　**City: Tuscola**　　　**County: Taylor**

Plan your trip: https://tpwd.texas.gov/state-parks/abilene

Activities:

- ❑ Archery
- ❑ Biking
- ❑ Boating
- ❑ Campfire
- ❑ Caving
- ❑ Disc Golf
- ❑ Fishing
- ❑ Geo Cache
- ❑ Golf
- ❑ Hiking
- ❑ Horseback
- ❑ Hunting
- ❑ Jr. Ranger
- ❑ Park Tours
- ❑ Rock Climbing
- ❑ Stargazing
- ❑ Swimming
- ❑ Wildlife & Birding
- ❑
- ❑

Facilities:

- ❑ ADA
- ❑ Gym
- ❑ Historic Sites
- ❑ Lodge
- ❑ Meeting hall
- ❑ Pavilions
- ❑ Picnic sites
- ❑ Pool
- ❑ Restrooms
- ❑ Showers
- ❑ Visitor center
- ❑ RV Camp
- ❑ Tent Camp
- ❑ Yurt Camp
- ❑ Cabins
- ❑ Lodge rooms
- ❑ Group barracks
- ❑ Screened shelter

Notes:

____

____

____

____

____

____

____

Get the Facts

- ❑ Phone (325) 572-3204
- ❑ Park Hours

____

- ❑ Reservations? ____Y ____N

date made_______________

- ❑ Open year 'round ___Y___N

dates___________________

- ❑ Check in time ___________
- ❑ Check out time __________
- ❑ Dog friendly _____Y _____N
- ❑ Max RV length __________
- ❑ Distance from home

miles: ________________

hours: ________________

- ❑ Address________________

____

____

Fees:

- ❑ Day Use $ ___________
- ❑ Camp Sites $ _________
- ❑ RV Sites $ ___________
- ❑ Refund policy

____

____

____

Make It Personal

Trip dates: | The weather was:

Why I went:

How I got there: (circle all that apply)

I went with:

We stayed in (space, cabin # etc):

Most relaxing day:

Something funny:

Someone we met:

Best story told:

We liked this:

The best food:

Games played:

Something disappointing:

Next time I'll do this differently:

Atlanta State Park
State: Texas   City: Atlanta   County: Cass

Plan your trip: https://tpwd.texas.gov/state-parks/atlanta

Activities:

- ❑ Archery
- ❑ Biking
- ❑ Boating
- ❑ Campfire
- ❑ Caving
- ❑ Disc Golf
- ❑ Fishing
- ❑ Geo Cache
- ❑ Golf
- ❑ Hiking
- ❑ Horseback
- ❑ Hunting
- ❑ Jr. Ranger
- ❑ Park Tours
- ❑ Rock Climbing
- ❑ Stargazing
- ❑ Swimming
- ❑ Wildlife & Birding
- ❑
- ❑

Facilities:

- ❑ ADA
- ❑ Gym
- ❑ Historic Sites
- ❑ Lodge
- ❑ Meeting hall
- ❑ Pavilions
- ❑ Picnic sites
- ❑ Pool
- ❑ Restrooms
- ❑ Showers
- ❑ Visitor center
- ❑ RV Camp
- ❑ Tent Camp
- ❑ Yurt Camp
- ❑ Cabins
- ❑ Lodge rooms
- ❑ Group barracks
- ❑ Screened shelter

Get the Facts

- ❑ Phone (903) 796-6476
- ❑ Park Hours

  ____

- ❑ Reservations? ____Y ____N

  date made_______________

- ❑ Open year 'round ___Y___N

  dates___________________

- ❑ Check in time ___________
- ❑ Check out time __________
- ❑ Dog friendly _____Y _____N
- ❑ Max RV length __________
- ❑ Distance from home

  miles: _________________

  hours: _________________

- ❑ Address________________

  ____

  ____

Fees:

- ❑ Day Use $ ___________
- ❑ Camp Sites $ _________
- ❑ RV Sites $ ___________
- ❑ Refund policy

  ____

  ____

  ____

Notes:

____

____

____

____

____

____

____

____

Make It Personal

Trip dates: | The weather was:

Why I went:

How I got there: (circle all that apply)

I went with:

We stayed in (space, cabin # etc):

Most relaxing day:

Something funny:

Someone we met:

Best story told:

We liked this:

The best food:

Games played:

Something disappointing:

Next time I'll do this differently:

Balmorhea State Park

State: Texas   City: Toyahvale   County: Reeves

Plan your trip: https://tpwd.texas.gov/state-parks/balmorhea

Activities:

- ❑ Archery
- ❑ Biking
- ❑ Boating
- ❑ Campfire
- ❑ Caving
- ❑ Disc Golf
- ❑ Fishing
- ❑ Geo Cache
- ❑ Golf
- ❑ Hiking
- ❑ Horseback
- ❑ Hunting
- ❑ Jr. Ranger
- ❑ Park Tours
- ❑ Rock Climbing
- ❑ Stargazing
- ❑ Swimming
- ❑ Wildlife & Birding
- ❑
- ❑

Facilities:

- ❑ ADA
- ❑ Gym
- ❑ Historic Sites
- ❑ Lodge
- ❑ Meeting hall
- ❑ Pavilions
- ❑ Picnic sites
- ❑ Pool
- ❑ Restrooms
- ❑ Showers
- ❑ Visitor center
- ❑ RV Camp
- ❑ Tent Camp
- ❑ Yurt Camp
- ❑ Cabins
- ❑ Lodge rooms
- ❑ Group barracks
- ❑ Screened shelter

Notes:

____

____

____

____

____

____

____

____

Get the Facts

- ❑ Phone (432) 375-2370
- ❑ Park Hours

____

- ❑ Reservations? _____Y _____N

date made________________

- ❑ Open year 'round ___Y___N

dates__________________

- ❑ Check in time ___________
- ❑ Check out time __________
- ❑ Dog friendly ______Y _____N
- ❑ Max RV length __________
- ❑ Distance from home

miles: __________________

hours: __________________

- ❑ Address________________

____

____

Fees:

- ❑ Day Use $ ___________
- ❑ Camp Sites $ _________
- ❑ RV Sites $ ___________
- ❑ Refund policy

____

____

____

Make It Personal

Trip dates: | The weather was:

Why I went:

How I got there: (circle all that apply)

I went with:

We stayed in (space, cabin # etc):

Most relaxing day:

Something funny:

Someone we met:

Best story told:

We liked this:

The best food:

Games played:

Something disappointing:

Next time I'll do this differently:

Bastrop State Park

State: Texas   City: Bastrop   County: Bastrop

Plan your trip: https://tpwd.texas.gov/state-parks/bastrop

Activities:

- ❑ Archery
- ❑ Biking
- ❑ Boating
- ❑ Campfire
- ❑ Caving
- ❑ Disc Golf
- ❑ Fishing
- ❑ Geo Cache
- ❑ Golf
- ❑ Hiking
- ❑ Horseback
- ❑ Hunting
- ❑ Jr. Ranger
- ❑ Park Tours
- ❑ Rock Climbing
- ❑ Stargazing
- ❑ Swimming
- ❑ Wildlife & Birding
- ❑
- ❑

Facilities:

- ❑ ADA
- ❑ Gym
- ❑ Historic Sites
- ❑ Lodge
- ❑ Meeting hall
- ❑ Pavilions
- ❑ Picnic sites
- ❑ Pool
- ❑ Restrooms
- ❑ Showers
- ❑ Visitor center
- ❑ RV Camp
- ❑ Tent Camp
- ❑ Yurt Camp
- ❑ Cabins
- ❑ Lodge rooms
- ❑ Group barracks
- ❑ Screened shelter

Notes:

____

____

____

____

____

____

____

____

Get the Facts

- ❑ Phone (512) 321-2101
- ❑ Park Hours

  ____

- ❑ Reservations? ____Y ____N

  date made_______________

- ❑ Open year 'round ___Y___N

  dates___________________

- ❑ Check in time ___________
- ❑ Check out time __________
- ❑ Dog friendly _____Y _____N
- ❑ Max RV length __________
- ❑ Distance from home

  miles: _________________

  hours: _________________

- ❑ Address_______________

  ____

Fees:

- ❑ Day Use $ ___________
- ❑ Camp Sites $ _________
- ❑ RV Sites $ ___________
- ❑ Refund policy

  ____

  ____

  ____

Make It Personal

Trip dates: | The weather was:

Why I went:

How I got there: (circle all that apply)

I went with:

We stayed in (space, cabin # etc):

Most relaxing day:

Something funny:

Someone we met:

Best story told:

We liked this:

The best food:

Games played:

Something disappointing:

Next time I'll do this differently:

Bentsen-Rio Grande Valley State Park

State: Texas   City: Mission   County: Hidalgo

Plan your trip: https://tpwd.texas.gov/state-parks/bentsen-rio-grande-valley

Activities:

- ❑ Archery
- ❑ Biking
- ❑ Boating
- ❑ Campfire
- ❑ Caving
- ❑ Disc Golf
- ❑ Fishing
- ❑ Geo Cache
- ❑ Golf
- ❑ Hiking
- ❑ Horseback
- ❑ Hunting
- ❑ Jr. Ranger
- ❑ Park Tours
- ❑ Rock Climbing
- ❑ Stargazing
- ❑ Swimming
- ❑ Wildlife & Birding
- ❑
- ❑

Facilities:

- ❑ ADA
- ❑ Gym
- ❑ Historic Sites
- ❑ Lodge
- ❑ Meeting hall
- ❑ Pavilions
- ❑ Picnic sites
- ❑ Pool
- ❑ Restrooms
- ❑ Showers
- ❑ Visitor center
- ❑ RV Camp
- ❑ Tent Camp
- ❑ Yurt Camp
- ❑ Cabins
- ❑ Lodge rooms
- ❑ Group barracks
- ❑ Screened shelter

Get the Facts

- ❑ Phone (956) 584-9156
- ❑ Park Hours

  ____

- ❑ Reservations? ____Y ____N

  date made______________

- ❑ Open year 'round ___Y___N

  dates__________________

- ❑ Check in time ___________
- ❑ Check out time __________
- ❑ Dog friendly _____Y _____N
- ❑ Max RV length __________
- ❑ Distance from home

  miles: ________________

  hours: ________________

- ❑ Address________________

  ____

  ____

Notes:

____

____

____

____

____

____

____

Fees:

- ❑ Day Use $ ___________
- ❑ Camp Sites $ _________
- ❑ RV Sites $ __________
- ❑ Refund policy

  ____

  ____

  ____

Make It Personal

Trip dates:

The weather was:

Why I went:

How I got there: (circle all that apply)

I went with:

We stayed in (space, cabin # etc):

Most relaxing day:

Something funny:

Someone we met:

Best story told:

We liked this:

The best food:

Games played:

Something disappointing:

Next time I'll do this differently:

Big Bend Ranch State Park
State: Texas   City: Marfa   County: Presidio

Plan your trip: https://tpwd.texas.gov/state-parks/big-bend-ranch

Activities:

- ❑ Archery
- ❑ Biking
- ❑ Boating
- ❑ Campfire
- ❑ Caving
- ❑ Disc Golf
- ❑ Fishing
- ❑ Geo Cache
- ❑ Golf
- ❑ Hiking
- ❑ Horseback
- ❑ Hunting
- ❑ Jr. Ranger
- ❑ Park Tours
- ❑ Rock Climbing
- ❑ Stargazing
- ❑ Swimming
- ❑ Wildlife & Birding
- ❑
- ❑

Facilities:

- ❑ ADA
- ❑ Gym
- ❑ Historic Sites
- ❑ Lodge
- ❑ Meeting hall
- ❑ Pavilions
- ❑ Picnic sites
- ❑ Pool
- ❑ Restrooms
- ❑ Showers
- ❑ Visitor center
- ❑ RV Camp
- ❑ Tent Camp
- ❑ Yurt Camp
- ❑ Cabins
- ❑ Lodge rooms
- ❑ Group barracks
- ❑ Screened shelter

Notes:

____

____

____

____

____

____

____

____

Get the Facts

- ❑ Phone (432) 263-4931
- ❑ Park Hours

____

- ❑ Reservations? _____Y _____N

date made_______________

- ❑ Open year 'round ___Y___N

dates__________________

- ❑ Check in time ___________
- ❑ Check out time __________
- ❑ Dog friendly _____Y _____N
- ❑ Max RV length __________
- ❑ Distance from home

miles: ________________

hours: ________________

- ❑ Address________________

____

____

Fees:

- ❑ Day Use $ ___________
- ❑ Camp Sites $ _________
- ❑ RV Sites $ __________
- ❑ Refund policy

____

____

____

Make It Personal

Trip dates:

The weather was:

Why I went:

How I got there: (circle all that apply)

I went with:

We stayed in (space, cabin # etc):

Most relaxing day:

Something funny:

Someone we met:

Best story told:

We liked this:

The best food:

Games played:

Something disappointing:

Next time I'll do this differently:

Big Spring State Park
State: Texas   City: Big Spring   County: Howard

Plan your trip: https://tpwd.texas.gov/state-parks/big-spring

Activities:

- ❑ Archery
- ❑ Biking
- ❑ Boating
- ❑ Campfire
- ❑ Caving
- ❑ Disc Golf
- ❑ Fishing
- ❑ Geo Cache
- ❑ Golf
- ❑ Hiking
- ❑ Horseback
- ❑ Hunting
- ❑ Jr. Ranger
- ❑ Park Tours
- ❑ Rock Climbing
- ❑ Stargazing
- ❑ Swimming
- ❑ Wildlife & Birding
- ❑
- ❑

Facilities:

- ❑ ADA
- ❑ Gym
- ❑ Historic Sites
- ❑ Lodge
- ❑ Meeting hall
- ❑ Pavilions
- ❑ Picnic sites
- ❑ Pool
- ❑ Restrooms
- ❑ Showers
- ❑ Visitor center
- ❑ RV Camp
- ❑ Tent Camp
- ❑ Yurt Camp
- ❑ Cabins
- ❑ Lodge rooms
- ❑ Group barracks
- ❑ Screened shelter

Notes:

____

____

____

____

____

____

____

____

____

Get the Facts

- ❑ Phone (432) 263-4931
- ❑ Park Hours

  ____

- ❑ Reservations? _____Y _____N

  date made_______________

- ❑ Open year 'round ___Y___N

  dates__________________

- ❑ Check in time ____________

- ❑ Check out time ___________

- ❑ Dog friendly ______Y ______N

- ❑ Max RV length ___________

- ❑ Distance from home

  miles: __________________

  hours: __________________

- ❑ Address________________

  ____

  ____

Fees:

- ❑ Day Use $ ____________
- ❑ Camp Sites $ __________
- ❑ RV Sites $ ____________
- ❑ Refund policy

  ____

  ____

  ____

Make It Personal

Trip dates: The weather was:

Why I went:

How I got there: (circle all that apply)

I went with:

We stayed in (space, cabin # etc):

Most relaxing day:

Something funny:

Someone we met:

Best story told:

We liked this:

The best food:

Games played:

Something disappointing:

Next time I'll do this differently:

Blanco State Park

State: Texas   City: Blanco   County: Blanco

Plan your trip: https://tpwd.texas.gov/state-parks/blanco

Activities:

- ❑ Archery
- ❑ Biking
- ❑ Boating
- ❑ Campfire
- ❑ Caving
- ❑ Disc Golf
- ❑ Fishing
- ❑ Geo Cache
- ❑ Golf
- ❑ Hiking
- ❑ Horseback
- ❑ Hunting
- ❑ Jr. Ranger
- ❑ Park Tours
- ❑ Rock Climbing
- ❑ Stargazing
- ❑ Swimming
- ❑ Wildlife & Birding
- ❑
- ❑

Facilities:

- ❑ ADA
- ❑ Gym
- ❑ Historic Sites
- ❑ Lodge
- ❑ Meeting hall
- ❑ Pavilions
- ❑ Picnic sites
- ❑ Pool
- ❑ Restrooms
- ❑ Showers
- ❑ Visitor center
- ❑ RV Camp
- ❑ Tent Camp
- ❑ Yurt Camp
- ❑ Cabins
- ❑ Lodge rooms
- ❑ Group barracks
- ❑ Screened shelter

Notes:

____

____

____

____

____

____

____

____

____

Get the Facts

- ❑ Phone (830) 833-4333
- ❑ Park Hours

____

- ❑ Reservations? _____Y _____N

date made______________

- ❑ Open year 'round ___Y___N

dates__________________

- ❑ Check in time ___________
- ❑ Check out time __________
- ❑ Dog friendly _____Y _____N
- ❑ Max RV length __________
- ❑ Distance from home

miles: ________________

hours: ________________

- ❑ Address________________

____

____

Fees:

- ❑ Day Use $ __________
- ❑ Camp Sites $ ________
- ❑ RV Sites $ __________
- ❑ Refund policy

____

____

____

Make It Personal

Trip dates: | The weather was:

Why I went:

How I got there: (circle all that apply)

I went with:

We stayed in (space, cabin # etc):

Most relaxing day:

Something funny:

Someone we met:

Best story told:

We liked this:

The best food:

Games played:

Something disappointing:

Next time I'll do this differently:

Bonham State Park

State: Texas   City: Bonham   County: Fannin

Plan your trip: https://tpwd.texas.gov/state-parks/blanco

Activities:

- ❑ Archery
- ❑ Biking
- ❑ Boating
- ❑ Campfire
- ❑ Caving
- ❑ Disc Golf
- ❑ Fishing
- ❑ Geo Cache
- ❑ Golf
- ❑ Hiking
- ❑ Horseback
- ❑ Hunting
- ❑ Jr. Ranger
- ❑ Park Tours
- ❑ Rock Climbing
- ❑ Stargazing
- ❑ Swimming
- ❑ Wildlife & Birding
- ❑
- ❑

Facilities:

- ❑ ADA
- ❑ Gym
- ❑ Historic Sites
- ❑ Lodge
- ❑ Meeting hall
- ❑ Pavilions
- ❑ Picnic sites
- ❑ Pool
- ❑ Restrooms
- ❑ Showers
- ❑ Visitor center
- ❑ RV Camp
- ❑ Tent Camp
- ❑ Yurt Camp
- ❑ Cabins
- ❑ Lodge rooms
- ❑ Group barracks
- ❑ Screened shelter

Notes:

____

____

____

____

____

____

____

____

Get the Facts

- ❑ Phone (830) 833-4333
- ❑ Park Hours

  ____

- ❑ Reservations? _____Y _____N

  date made_______________

- ❑ Open year 'round ___Y___N

  dates__________________

- ❑ Check in time ____________

- ❑ Check out time ___________

- ❑ Dog friendly ______Y ______N

- ❑ Max RV length ___________

- ❑ Distance from home

  miles: _______________________

  hours: _______________________

- ❑ Address_________________

  ____

  ____

Fees:

- ❑ Day Use $ ___________
- ❑ Camp Sites $ _________
- ❑ RV Sites $ ___________
- ❑ Refund policy

  ____

  ____

  ____

Make It Personal

Trip dates: | The weather was:

Why I went:

How I got there: (circle all that apply)

I went with:

We stayed in (space, cabin # etc):

Most relaxing day:

Something funny:

Someone we met:

Best story told:

We liked this:

The best food:

Games played:

Something disappointing:

Next time I'll do this differently:

Brazos Bend State Park
State: Texas   City: Needville   County: Fort Bend

Plan your trip: https://tpwd.texas.gov/state-parks/brazos-bend

Activities:

- ❏ Archery
- ❏ Biking
- ❏ Boating
- ❏ Campfire
- ❏ Caving
- ❏ Disc Golf
- ❏ Fishing
- ❏ Geo Cache
- ❏ Golf
- ❏ Hiking
- ❏ Horseback
- ❏ Hunting
- ❏ Jr. Ranger
- ❏ Park Tours
- ❏ Rock Climbing
- ❏ Stargazing
- ❏ Swimming
- ❏ Wildlife & Birding
- ❏
- ❏

Facilities:

- ❏ ADA
- ❏ Gym
- ❏ Historic Sites
- ❏ Lodge
- ❏ Meeting hall
- ❏ Pavilions
- ❏ Picnic sites
- ❏ Pool
- ❏ Restrooms
- ❏ Showers
- ❏ Visitor center
- ❏ RV Camp
- ❏ Tent Camp
- ❏ Yurt Camp
- ❏ Cabins
- ❏ Lodge rooms
- ❏ Group barracks
- ❏ Screened shelter

Notes:

____

____

____

____

____

____

____

____

____

Get the Facts

- ❏ Phone (979) 553-5102
- ❏ Park Hours

____

- ❏ Reservations? ____Y ____N

date made______________

- ❏ Open year 'round ___Y___N

dates__________________

- ❏ Check in time ___________
- ❏ Check out time __________
- ❏ Dog friendly _____Y _____N
- ❏ Max RV length __________
- ❏ Distance from home

miles: ________________

hours: ________________

- ❏ Address________________

____

____

Fees:

- ❏ Day Use $ ___________
- ❏ Camp Sites $ _________
- ❏ RV Sites $ ___________
- ❏ Refund policy

____

____

____

Make It Personal

Trip dates: ______________________ | The weather was:

Why I went: ____

How I got there: (circle all that apply)

I went with: ____

We stayed in (space, cabin # etc): _________________________

Most relaxing day: ____

Something funny: ____

Someone we met: ____

Best story told: ____

We liked this: ____

The best food: ____

Games played: ____

Something disappointing: ___________________________________

Next time I'll do this differently: ________________________

Buescher State Park
State: Texas   City: Smithville   County: Bastrop

Plan your trip: https://tpwd.texas.gov/state-parks/buescher

Activities:

- ❑ Archery
- ❑ Biking
- ❑ Boating
- ❑ Campfire
- ❑ Caving
- ❑ Disc Golf
- ❑ Fishing
- ❑ Geo Cache
- ❑ Golf
- ❑ Hiking
- ❑ Horseback
- ❑ Hunting
- ❑ Jr. Ranger
- ❑ Park Tours
- ❑ Rock Climbing
- ❑ Stargazing
- ❑ Swimming
- ❑ Wildlife & Birding
- ❑
- ❑

Facilities:

- ❑ ADA
- ❑ Gym
- ❑ Historic Sites
- ❑ Lodge
- ❑ Meeting hall
- ❑ Pavilions
- ❑ Picnic sites
- ❑ Pool
- ❑ Restrooms
- ❑ Showers
- ❑ Visitor center
- ❑ RV Camp
- ❑ Tent Camp
- ❑ Yurt Camp
- ❑ Cabins
- ❑ Lodge rooms
- ❑ Group barracks
- ❑ Screened shelter

Notes:

____

____

____

____

____

____

____

Get the Facts

- ❑ Phone (512) 237-2241
- ❑ Park Hours

____

- ❑ Reservations? _____Y _____N

date made_______________

- ❑ Open year 'round ___Y___N

dates____________________

- ❑ Check in time ____________
- ❑ Check out time ___________
- ❑ Dog friendly ______Y _____N
- ❑ Max RV length ___________
- ❑ Distance from home

miles: _________________

hours: _________________

- ❑ Address________________

____

____

Fees:

- ❑ Day Use $ ___________
- ❑ Camp Sites $ _________
- ❑ RV Sites $ ___________
- ❑ Refund policy

____

____

Make It Personal

Trip dates: | **The weather was:**

Why I went:

How I got there: (circle all that apply)

I went with:

We stayed in (space, cabin # etc):

Most relaxing day:

Something funny:

Someone we met:

Best story told:

We liked this:

The best food:

Games played:

Something disappointing:

Next time I'll do this differently:

Caddo Lake State Park

State: Texas   City: Karnack   County: Harrison

Plan your trip: https://tpwd.texas.gov/state-parks/caddo-lake

Activities:

- ❑ Archery
- ❑ Biking
- ❑ Boating
- ❑ Campfire
- ❑ Caving
- ❑ Disc Golf
- ❑ Fishing
- ❑ Geo Cache
- ❑ Golf
- ❑ Hiking
- ❑ Horseback
- ❑ Hunting
- ❑ Jr. Ranger
- ❑ Park Tours
- ❑ Rock Climbing
- ❑ Stargazing
- ❑ Swimming
- ❑ Wildlife & Birding
- ❑
- ❑

Facilities:

- ❑ ADA
- ❑ Gym
- ❑ Historic Sites
- ❑ Lodge
- ❑ Meeting hall
- ❑ Pavilions
- ❑ Picnic sites
- ❑ Pool
- ❑ Restrooms
- ❑ Showers
- ❑ Visitor center
- ❑ RV Camp
- ❑ Tent Camp
- ❑ Yurt Camp
- ❑ Cabins
- ❑ Lodge rooms
- ❑ Group barracks
- ❑ Screened shelter

Notes:

____

____

____

____

____

____

____

____

____

Get the Facts

- ❑ Phone (903) 679-3351
- ❑ Park Hours

  ____

- ❑ Reservations? ____Y ____N

  date made______________
- ❑ Open year 'round ___Y___N

  dates__________________
- ❑ Check in time ___________
- ❑ Check out time __________
- ❑ Dog friendly _____Y _____N
- ❑ Max RV length __________
- ❑ Distance from home

  miles: ________________

  hours: ________________
- ❑ Address________________

  ____

  ____

Fees:

- ❑ Day Use $ __________
- ❑ Camp Sites $ ________
- ❑ RV Sites $ __________
- ❑ Refund policy

  ____

  ____

  ____

Make It Personal

Trip dates: _______________________ | The weather was:

Why I went: ____

How I got there: (circle all that apply)

I went with: ____

We stayed in (space, cabin # etc): ___________________________

Most relaxing day: _______________________________________

Something funny: ____

Someone we met: ____

Best story told: ____

We liked this: ____

The best food: ____

Games played: ____

Something disappointing: __________________________________

Next time I'll do this differently: ___________________________

Caprock Canyons State Park & Trailway

State: Texas   City: Quitaque   County: Briscoe

Plan your trip: https://tpwd.texas.gov/state-parks/caprock-canyons

Activities:

- ❑ Archery
- ❑ Biking
- ❑ Boating
- ❑ Campfire
- ❑ Caving
- ❑ Disc Golf
- ❑ Fishing
- ❑ Geo Cache
- ❑ Golf
- ❑ Hiking
- ❑ Horseback
- ❑ Hunting
- ❑ Jr. Ranger
- ❑ Park Tours
- ❑ Rock Climbing
- ❑ Stargazing
- ❑ Swimming
- ❑ Wildlife & Birding
- ❑
- ❑

Facilities:

- ❑ ADA
- ❑ Gym
- ❑ Historic Sites
- ❑ Lodge
- ❑ Meeting hall
- ❑ Pavilions
- ❑ Picnic sites
- ❑ Pool
- ❑ Restrooms
- ❑ Showers
- ❑ Visitor center
- ❑ RV Camp
- ❑ Tent Camp
- ❑ Yurt Camp
- ❑ Cabins
- ❑ Lodge rooms
- ❑ Group barracks
- ❑ Screened shelter

Get the Facts

- ❑ Phone (806) 455-1492
- ❑ Park Hours

  ____

- ❑ Reservations? _____Y _____N

  date made_______________
- ❑ Open year 'round ___Y___N

  dates__________________
- ❑ Check in time ___________
- ❑ Check out time __________
- ❑ Dog friendly _____Y _____N
- ❑ Max RV length __________
- ❑ Distance from home

  miles: _________________

  hours: _________________
- ❑ Address________________

  ____

  ____

Fees:

- ❑ Day Use $ ___________
- ❑ Camp Sites $ _________
- ❑ RV Sites $ ___________
- ❑ Refund policy

  ____

  ____

  ____

Notes:

____

____

____

____

____

____

____

____

Make It Personal

Trip dates: | The weather was:

Why I went:

How I got there: (circle all that apply)

I went with:

We stayed in (space, cabin # etc):

Most relaxing day:

Something funny:

Someone we met:

Best story told:

We liked this:

The best food:

Games played:

Something disappointing:

Next time I'll do this differently:

Cedar Hills State Park

State: Texas   City: Cedar Hill   County: Dallas

Plan your trip: https://tpwd.texas.gov/state-parks/cedar-hill

Activities:

- ❑ Archery
- ❑ Biking
- ❑ Boating
- ❑ Campfire
- ❑ Caving
- ❑ Disc Golf
- ❑ Fishing
- ❑ Geo Cache
- ❑ Golf
- ❑ Hiking
- ❑ Horseback
- ❑ Hunting
- ❑ Jr. Ranger
- ❑ Park Tours
- ❑ Rock Climbing
- ❑ Stargazing
- ❑ Swimming
- ❑ Wildlife & Birding
- ❑
- ❑

Facilities:

- ❑ ADA
- ❑ Gym
- ❑ Historic Sites
- ❑ Lodge
- ❑ Meeting hall
- ❑ Pavilions
- ❑ Picnic sites
- ❑ Pool
- ❑ Restrooms
- ❑ Showers
- ❑ Visitor center
- ❑ RV Camp
- ❑ Tent Camp
- ❑ Yurt Camp
- ❑ Cabins
- ❑ Lodge rooms
- ❑ Group barracks
- ❑ Screened shelter

Notes:

____

____

____

____

____

____

____

____

Get the Facts

- ❑ Phone (972) 291-3900
- ❑ Park Hours

____

- ❑ Reservations? _____Y _____N

date made_______________

- ❑ Open year 'round ___Y___N

dates___________________

- ❑ Check in time ____________
- ❑ Check out time ___________
- ❑ Dog friendly ______Y ______N
- ❑ Max RV length ___________
- ❑ Distance from home

miles: ___________________

hours: ___________________

- ❑ Address________________

____

____

Fees:

- ❑ Day Use $ ___________
- ❑ Camp Sites $ _________
- ❑ RV Sites $ ___________
- ❑ Refund policy

____

____

____

Make It Personal

Trip dates:

The weather was:

Why I went:

How I got there: (circle all that apply)

I went with:

We stayed in (space, cabin # etc):

Most relaxing day:

Something funny:

Someone we met:

Best story told:

We liked this:

The best food:

Games played:

Something disappointing:

Next time I'll do this differently:

Choke Canyon State Park

State: Texas   **City: Calliham**   **County: McMullen**

Plan your trip: https://tpwd.texas.gov/state-parks/choke-canyon

Activities:

- ❑ Archery
- ❑ Biking
- ❑ Boating
- ❑ Campfire
- ❑ Caving
- ❑ Disc Golf
- ❑ Fishing
- ❑ Geo Cache
- ❑ Golf
- ❑ Hiking
- ❑ Horseback
- ❑ Hunting
- ❑ Jr. Ranger
- ❑ Park Tours
- ❑ Rock Climbing
- ❑ Stargazing
- ❑ Swimming
- ❑ Wildlife & Birding
- ❑
- ❑

Facilities:

- ❑ ADA
- ❑ Gym
- ❑ Historic Sites
- ❑ Lodge
- ❑ Meeting hall
- ❑ Pavilions
- ❑ Picnic sites
- ❑ Pool
- ❑ Restrooms
- ❑ Showers
- ❑ Visitor center
- ❑ RV Camp
- ❑ Tent Camp
- ❑ Yurt Camp
- ❑ Cabins
- ❑ Lodge rooms
- ❑ Group barracks
- ❑ Screened shelter

Notes:

____
____
____
____
____
____
____
____
____
____
____
____
____

Get the Facts

- ❑ Phone (361) 786-3868
- ❑ Park Hours

  ____

- ❑ Reservations? _____Y _____N

  date made_______________

- ❑ Open year 'round ___Y___N

  dates_________________

- ❑ Check in time ___________
- ❑ Check out time ___________
- ❑ Dog friendly ______Y ______N
- ❑ Max RV length ___________
- ❑ Distance from home

  miles: ________________

  hours: ________________

- ❑ Address_______________

  ____

  ____

Fees:

- ❑ Day Use $ ___________
- ❑ Camp Sites $ _________
- ❑ RV Sites $ ___________
- ❑ Refund policy

  ____

  ____

Make It Personal

Trip dates: | The weather was:

Why I went:

How I got there: (circle all that apply)

I went with:

We stayed in (space, cabin # etc):

Most relaxing day:

Something funny:

Someone we met:

Best story told:

We liked this:

The best food:

Games played:

Something disappointing:

Next time I'll do this differently:

Cleburne State Park

State: Texas **City: Cleburne** **County: Johnson**

Plan your trip: https://tpwd.texas.gov/state-parks/cleburne

Activities:

- ❏ Archery
- ❏ Biking
- ❏ Boating
- ❏ Campfire
- ❏ Caving
- ❏ Disc Golf
- ❏ Fishing
- ❏ Geo Cache
- ❏ Golf
- ❏ Hiking
- ❏ Horseback
- ❏ Hunting
- ❏ Jr. Ranger
- ❏ Park Tours
- ❏ Rock Climbing
- ❏ Stargazing
- ❏ Swimming
- ❏ Wildlife & Birding
- ❏
- ❏

Facilities:

- ❏ ADA
- ❏ Gym
- ❏ Historic Sites
- ❏ Lodge
- ❏ Meeting hall
- ❏ Pavilions
- ❏ Picnic sites
- ❏ Pool
- ❏ Restrooms
- ❏ Showers
- ❏ Visitor center
- ❏ RV Camp
- ❏ Tent Camp
- ❏ Yurt Camp
- ❏ Cabins
- ❏ Lodge rooms
- ❏ Group barracks
- ❏ Screened shelter

Notes:

____

____

____

____

____

____

____

____

Get the Facts

- ❏ Phone (817) 645-4215
- ❏ Park Hours

____

- ❏ Reservations? ____Y ____N

date made_______________

- ❏ Open year 'round ___Y___N

dates___________________

- ❏ Check in time ___________
- ❏ Check out time __________
- ❏ Dog friendly _____Y _____N
- ❏ Max RV length __________
- ❏ Distance from home

miles: ________________

hours: ________________

- ❏ Address________________

____

____

Fees:

- ❏ Day Use $ __________
- ❏ Camp Sites $ ________
- ❏ RV Sites $ __________
- ❏ Refund policy

____

____

____

Make It Personal

Trip dates: | The weather was:

Why I went:

How I got there: (circle all that apply)

I went with:

We stayed in (space, cabin # etc):

Most relaxing day:

Something funny:

Someone we met:

Best story told:

We liked this:

The best food:

Games played:

Something disappointing:

Next time I'll do this differently:

Colorado Bend State Park

State: Texas   City: Bend   County: San Saba

Plan your trip: https://tpwd.texas.gov/state-parks/colorado-bend

Activities:

- ❑ Archery
- ❑ Biking
- ❑ Boating
- ❑ Campfire
- ❑ Caving
- ❑ Disc Golf
- ❑ Fishing
- ❑ Geo Cache
- ❑ Golf
- ❑ Hiking
- ❑ Horseback
- ❑ Hunting
- ❑ Jr. Ranger
- ❑ Park Tours
- ❑ Rock Climbing
- ❑ Stargazing
- ❑ Swimming
- ❑ Wildlife & Birding
- ❑
- ❑

Facilities:

- ❑ ADA
- ❑ Gym
- ❑ Historic Sites
- ❑ Lodge
- ❑ Meeting hall
- ❑ Pavilions
- ❑ Picnic sites
- ❑ Pool
- ❑ Restrooms
- ❑ Showers
- ❑ Visitor center
- ❑ RV Camp
- ❑ Tent Camp
- ❑ Yurt Camp
- ❑ Cabins
- ❑ Lodge rooms
- ❑ Group barracks
- ❑ Screened shelter

Notes:

____

____

____

____

____

____

____

____

____

Get the Facts

- ❑ Phone (817) 645-4215
- ❑ Park Hours

  ____

- ❑ Reservations? _____Y _____N

  date made_______________

- ❑ Open year 'round ___Y___N

  dates_________________________

- ❑ Check in time _____________

- ❑ Check out time ___________

- ❑ Dog friendly _______Y ______N

- ❑ Max RV length ___________

- ❑ Distance from home

  miles: _______________________

  hours: _______________________

- ❑ Address__________________

  ____

  ____

Fees:

- ❑ Day Use $ ____________
- ❑ Camp Sites $ __________
- ❑ RV Sites $ ____________
- ❑ Refund policy

  ____

  ____

  ____

Make It Personal

Trip dates:

The weather was:

Why I went:

How I got there: (circle all that apply)

I went with:

We stayed in (space, cabin # etc):

Most relaxing day:

Something funny:

Someone we met:

Best story told:

We liked this:

The best food:

Games played:

Something disappointing:

Next time I'll do this differently:

Cooper Lake State Park - Doctors Creek

State: Texas   City: Cooper   County: Delta

Plan your trip: https://tpwd.texas.gov/state-parks/cooper-lake

Activities:

- ☐ Archery
- ☐ Biking
- ☐ Boating
- ☐ Campfire
- ☐ Caving
- ☐ Disc Golf
- ☐ Fishing
- ☐ Geo Cache
- ☐ Golf
- ☐ Hiking
- ☐ Horseback
- ☐ Hunting
- ☐ Jr. Ranger
- ☐ Park Tours
- ☐ Rock Climbing
- ☐ Stargazing
- ☐ Swimming
- ☐ Wildlife & Birding
- ☐
- ☐

Facilities:

- ☐ ADA
- ☐ Gym
- ☐ Historic Sites
- ☐ Lodge
- ☐ Meeting hall
- ☐ Pavilions
- ☐ Picnic sites
- ☐ Pool
- ☐ Restrooms
- ☐ Showers
- ☐ Visitor center
- ☐ RV Camp
- ☐ Tent Camp
- ☐ Yurt Camp
- ☐ Cabins
- ☐ Lodge rooms
- ☐ Group barracks
- ☐ Screened shelter

Notes:

____

____

____

____

____

____

____

____

Get the Facts

- ☐ Phone (903) 395-3100
- ☐ Park Hours

  ____

- ☐ Reservations? _____Y _____N

  date made_______________

- ☐ Open year 'round ___Y___N

  dates___________________

- ☐ Check in time ___________

- ☐ Check out time __________

- ☐ Dog friendly _____Y _____N

- ☐ Max RV length __________

- ☐ Distance from home

  miles: ________________

  hours: ________________

- ☐ Address________________

  ____

  ____

Fees:

- ☐ Day Use $ __________
- ☐ Camp Sites $ ________
- ☐ RV Sites $ __________
- ☐ Refund policy

  ____

  ____

  ____

Make It Personal

Trip dates: | The weather was:

Why I went:

How I got there: (circle all that apply)

I went with:

We stayed in (space, cabin # etc):

Most relaxing day:

Something funny:

Someone we met:

Best story told:

We liked this:

The best food:

Games played:

Something disappointing:

Next time I'll do this differently:

Cooper Lake State Park – South Sulphur

State: Texas   City: Cooper   County: Hopkins

Plan your trip: https://tpwd.texas.gov/state-parks/cooper-lake

Activities:

- ❑ Archery
- ❑ Biking
- ❑ Boating
- ❑ Campfire
- ❑ Caving
- ❑ Disc Golf
- ❑ Fishing
- ❑ Geo Cache
- ❑ Golf
- ❑ Hiking
- ❑ Horseback
- ❑ Hunting
- ❑ Jr. Ranger
- ❑ Park Tours
- ❑ Rock Climbing
- ❑ Stargazing
- ❑ Swimming
- ❑ Wildlife & Birding
- ❑
- ❑

Facilities:

- ❑ ADA
- ❑ Gym
- ❑ Historic Sites
- ❑ Lodge
- ❑ Meeting hall
- ❑ Pavilions
- ❑ Picnic sites
- ❑ Pool
- ❑ Restrooms
- ❑ Showers
- ❑ Visitor center
- ❑ RV Camp
- ❑ Tent Camp
- ❑ Yurt Camp
- ❑ Cabins
- ❑ Lodge rooms
- ❑ Group barracks
- ❑ Screened shelter

Notes:

____

____

____

____

____

____

____

____

____

Get the Facts

- ❑ Phone (903) 945-5256
- ❑ Park Hours

____

- ❑ Reservations? _____Y _____N

date made_______________

- ❑ Open year 'round ___Y___N

dates___________________

- ❑ Check in time ____________
- ❑ Check out time ___________
- ❑ Dog friendly ______Y ______N
- ❑ Max RV length ___________
- ❑ Distance from home

miles: _________________

hours: _________________

- ❑ Address________________

____

____

Fees:

- ❑ Day Use $ ___________
- ❑ Camp Sites $ _________
- ❑ RV Sites $ ___________
- ❑ Refund policy

____

____

Make It Personal

Trip dates: | The weather was:

Why I went:

How I got there: (circle all that apply)

I went with:

We stayed in (space, cabin # etc):

Most relaxing day:

Something funny:

Someone we met:

Best story told:

We liked this:

The best food:

Games played:

Something disappointing:

Next time I'll do this differently:

Copper Breaks State Park
State: Texas   City: Quanah   County: Hardeman

Plan your trip: https://tpwd.texas.gov/state-parks/copper-breaks

Activities:

- ❏ Archery
- ❏ Biking
- ❏ Boating
- ❏ Campfire
- ❏ Caving
- ❏ Disc Golf
- ❏ Fishing
- ❏ Geo Cache
- ❏ Golf
- ❏ Hiking
- ❏ Horseback
- ❏ Hunting
- ❏ Jr. Ranger
- ❏ Park Tours
- ❏ Rock Climbing
- ❏ Stargazing
- ❏ Swimming
- ❏ Wildlife & Birding
- ❏
- ❏

Facilities:

- ❏ ADA
- ❏ Gym
- ❏ Historic Sites
- ❏ Lodge
- ❏ Meeting hall
- ❏ Pavilions
- ❏ Picnic sites
- ❏ Pool
- ❏ Restrooms
- ❏ Showers
- ❏ Visitor center
- ❏ RV Camp
- ❏ Tent Camp
- ❏ Yurt Camp
- ❏ Cabins
- ❏ Lodge rooms
- ❏ Group barracks
- ❏ Screened shelter

Notes:

____

____

____

____

____

____

____

____

Get the Facts

- ❏ Phone (940) 839-4331
- ❏ Park Hours

  ____

- ❏ Reservations? _____Y _____N

  date made_______________

- ❏ Open year 'round ___Y___N

  dates__________________

- ❏ Check in time ___________
- ❏ Check out time __________
- ❏ Dog friendly ______Y ______N
- ❏ Max RV length __________
- ❏ Distance from home

  miles: __________________

  hours: __________________

- ❏ Address________________

  ____

  ____

Fees:

- ❏ Day Use $ ___________
- ❏ Camp Sites $ _________
- ❏ RV Sites $ __________
- ❏ Refund policy

  ____

  ____

Make It Personal

Trip dates: | The weather was:

Why I went:

How I got there: (circle all that apply)

I went with:

We stayed in (space, cabin # etc):

Most relaxing day:

Something funny:

Someone we met:

Best story told:

We liked this:

The best food:

Games played:

Something disappointing:

Next time I'll do this differently:

Daingerfield State Park
State: Texas   **City: Daingerfield**   **County: Morris**

Plan your trip: https://tpwd.texas.gov/state-parks/daingerfield

Activities:

- ❑ Archery
- ❑ Biking
- ❑ Boating
- ❑ Campfire
- ❑ Caving
- ❑ Disc Golf
- ❑ Fishing
- ❑ Geo Cache
- ❑ Golf
- ❑ Hiking
- ❑ Horseback
- ❑ Hunting
- ❑ Jr. Ranger
- ❑ Park Tours
- ❑ Rock Climbing
- ❑ Stargazing
- ❑ Swimming
- ❑ Wildlife & Birding
- ❑
- ❑

Facilities:

- ❑ ADA
- ❑ Gym
- ❑ Historic Sites
- ❑ Lodge
- ❑ Meeting hall
- ❑ Pavilions
- ❑ Picnic sites
- ❑ Pool
- ❑ Restrooms
- ❑ Showers
- ❑ Visitor center
- ❑ RV Camp
- ❑ Tent Camp
- ❑ Yurt Camp
- ❑ Cabins
- ❑ Lodge rooms
- ❑ Group barracks
- ❑ Screened shelter

Get the Facts

- ❑ Phone (903) 645-2921
- ❑ Park Hours

  ____

- ❑ Reservations? _____Y _____N

  date made_______________

- ❑ Open year 'round ___Y___N

  dates_________________

- ❑ Check in time ___________
- ❑ Check out time __________
- ❑ Dog friendly _____Y _____N
- ❑ Max RV length __________
- ❑ Distance from home

  miles: ________________

  hours: ________________

- ❑ Address_______________

  ____

  ____

Fees:

- ❑ Day Use $ __________
- ❑ Camp Sites $ _________
- ❑ RV Sites $ __________
- ❑ Refund policy

  ____

  ____

  ____

Notes:

____

____

____

____

____

____

____

____

____

Make It Personal

Trip dates: | The weather was:

Why I went:

How I got there: (circle all that apply)

I went with:

We stayed in (space, cabin # etc):

Most relaxing day:

Something funny:

Someone we met:

Best story told:

We liked this:

The best food:

Games played:

Something disappointing:

Next time I'll do this differently:

Davis Mountains State Park

State: Texas   City: Fort Davis   County: Jeff Davis

Plan your trip: https://tpwd.texas.gov/state-parks/davis-mountains

Activities:

- ❑ Archery
- ❑ Biking
- ❑ Boating
- ❑ Campfire
- ❑ Caving
- ❑ Disc Golf
- ❑ Fishing
- ❑ Geo Cache
- ❑ Golf
- ❑ Hiking
- ❑ Horseback
- ❑ Hunting
- ❑ Jr. Ranger
- ❑ Park Tours
- ❑ Rock Climbing
- ❑ Stargazing
- ❑ Swimming
- ❑ Wildlife & Birding
- ❑
- ❑

Facilities:

- ❑ ADA
- ❑ Gym
- ❑ Historic Sites
- ❑ Lodge
- ❑ Meeting hall
- ❑ Pavilions
- ❑ Picnic sites
- ❑ Pool
- ❑ Restrooms
- ❑ Showers
- ❑ Visitor center
- ❑ RV Camp
- ❑ Tent Camp
- ❑ Yurt Camp
- ❑ Cabins
- ❑ Lodge rooms
- ❑ Group barracks
- ❑ Screened shelter

Notes:

____

____

____

____

____

____

____

____

Get the Facts

- ❑ Phone (432) 426-3337
- ❑ Park Hours

____

- ❑ Reservations? _____Y _____N

    date made_______________

- ❑ Open year 'round ___Y___N

    dates___________________

- ❑ Check in time ____________

- ❑ Check out time ___________

- ❑ Dog friendly _____Y _____N

- ❑ Max RV length ___________

- ❑ Distance from home

    miles: _________________

    hours: _________________

- ❑ Address________________

____

____

Fees:

- ❑ Day Use $ ___________
- ❑ Camp Sites $ _________
- ❑ RV Sites $ ___________
- ❑ Refund policy

____

____

____

Make It Personal

Trip dates: | The weather was:

Why I went:

How I got there: (circle all that apply)

I went with:

We stayed in (space, cabin # etc):

Most relaxing day:

Something funny:

Someone we met:

Best story told:

We liked this:

The best food:

Games played:

Something disappointing:

Next time I'll do this differently:

Devils River State Natural Area

State: Texas   City: Del Rio   County: Val Verde

Plan your trip: https://tpwd.texas.gov/state-parks/devils-river

Activities:

- ❏ Archery
- ❏ Biking
- ❏ Boating
- ❏ Campfire
- ❏ Caving
- ❏ Disc Golf
- ❏ Fishing
- ❏ Geo Cache
- ❏ Golf
- ❏ Hiking
- ❏ Horseback
- ❏ Hunting
- ❏ Jr. Ranger
- ❏ Park Tours
- ❏ Rock Climbing
- ❏ Stargazing
- ❏ Swimming
- ❏ Wildlife & Birding
- ❏
- ❏

Facilities:

- ❏ ADA
- ❏ Gym
- ❏ Historic Sites
- ❏ Lodge
- ❏ Meeting hall
- ❏ Pavilions
- ❏ Picnic sites
- ❏ Pool
- ❏ Restrooms
- ❏ Showers
- ❏ Visitor center
- ❏ RV Camp
- ❏ Tent Camp
- ❏ Yurt Camp
- ❏ Cabins
- ❏ Lodge rooms
- ❏ Group barracks
- ❏ Screened shelter

Notes:

____

____

____

____

____

____

____

____

Get the Facts

- ❏ Phone (830) 395-2133
- ❏ Park Hours

____

- ❏ Reservations? _____Y _____N

date made_______________

- ❏ Open year 'round ___Y___N

dates___________________

- ❏ Check in time ____________
- ❏ Check out time ___________
- ❏ Dog friendly ______Y ______N
- ❏ Max RV length ___________
- ❏ Distance from home

miles: __________________

hours: __________________

- ❏ Address________________

____

____

Fees:

- ❏ Day Use $ ___________
- ❏ Camp Sites $ __________
- ❏ RV Sites $ ___________
- ❏ Refund policy

____

____

____

Make It Personal

Trip dates: | The weather was:

Why I went:

How I got there: (circle all that apply)

I went with:

We stayed in (space, cabin # etc):

Most relaxing day:

Something funny:

Someone we met:

Best story told:

We liked this:

The best food:

Games played:

Something disappointing:

Next time I'll do this differently:

Dinosaur Valley State Park
State: Texas   City: Glen Rose   County: Somervell

Plan your trip: https://tpwd.texas.gov/state-parks/dinosaur-valley

Activities:

- ❑ Archery
- ❑ Biking
- ❑ Boating
- ❑ Campfire
- ❑ Caving
- ❑ Disc Golf
- ❑ Fishing
- ❑ Geo Cache
- ❑ Golf
- ❑ Hiking
- ❑ Horseback
- ❑ Hunting
- ❑ Jr. Ranger
- ❑ Park Tours
- ❑ Rock Climbing
- ❑ Stargazing
- ❑ Swimming
- ❑ Wildlife & Birding
- ❑
- ❑

Facilities:

- ❑ ADA
- ❑ Gym
- ❑ Historic Sites
- ❑ Lodge
- ❑ Meeting hall
- ❑ Pavilions
- ❑ Picnic sites
- ❑ Pool
- ❑ Restrooms
- ❑ Showers
- ❑ Visitor center
- ❑ RV Camp
- ❑ Tent Camp
- ❑ Yurt Camp
- ❑ Cabins
- ❑ Lodge rooms
- ❑ Group barracks
- ❑ Screened shelter

Notes:

____

____

____

____

____

____

____

____

____

Get the Facts

- ❑ Phone (254) 897-4588
- ❑ Park Hours

____

- ❑ Reservations? _____Y _____N

date made_______________

- ❑ Open year 'round ___Y___N

dates___________________

- ❑ Check in time ____________
- ❑ Check out time ___________
- ❑ Dog friendly ______Y ______N
- ❑ Max RV length ___________
- ❑ Distance from home

miles: __________________

hours: __________________

- ❑ Address_________________

____

____

Fees:

- ❑ Day Use $ ____________
- ❑ Camp Sites $ _________
- ❑ RV Sites $ ___________
- ❑ Refund policy

____

____

____

Make It Personal

Trip dates: | The weather was:

Why I went:

How I got there: (circle all that apply)

I went with:

We stayed in (space, cabin # etc):

Most relaxing day:

Something funny:

Someone we met:

Best story told:

We liked this:

The best food:

Games played:

Something disappointing:

Next time I'll do this differently:

Eisenhower State Park

State: Texas   City: Denison   County: Grayson

Plan your trip: https://tpwd.texas.gov/state-parks/eisenhower

Activities:

- ❑ Archery
- ❑ Biking
- ❑ Boating
- ❑ Campfire
- ❑ Caving
- ❑ Disc Golf
- ❑ Fishing
- ❑ Geo Cache
- ❑ Golf
- ❑ Hiking
- ❑ Horseback
- ❑ Hunting
- ❑ Jr. Ranger
- ❑ Park Tours
- ❑ Rock Climbing
- ❑ Stargazing
- ❑ Swimming
- ❑ Wildlife & Birding
- ❑
- ❑

Facilities:

- ❑ ADA
- ❑ Gym
- ❑ Historic Sites
- ❑ Lodge
- ❑ Meeting hall
- ❑ Pavilions
- ❑ Picnic sites
- ❑ Pool
- ❑ Restrooms
- ❑ Showers
- ❑ Visitor center
- ❑ RV Camp
- ❑ Tent Camp
- ❑ Yurt Camp
- ❑ Cabins
- ❑ Lodge rooms
- ❑ Group barracks
- ❑ Screened shelter

Notes:

____
____
____
____
____
____
____
____
____
____
____
____

Get the Facts

- ❑ Phone (903) 465-1956
- ❑ Park Hours

____

- ❑ Reservations? _____Y _____N

date made_______________

- ❑ Open year 'round ___Y___N

dates__________________

- ❑ Check in time ____________
- ❑ Check out time ___________
- ❑ Dog friendly _______Y _______N
- ❑ Max RV length ___________
- ❑ Distance from home

miles: ___________________

hours: ___________________

- ❑ Address_________________

____

____

Fees:

- ❑ Day Use $ ____________
- ❑ Camp Sites $ _________
- ❑ RV Sites $ ___________
- ❑ Refund policy

____

____

Make It Personal

Trip dates: | The weather was:

Why I went:

How I got there: (circle all that apply)

I went with:

We stayed in (space, cabin # etc):

Most relaxing day:

Something funny:

Someone we met:

Best story told:

We liked this:

The best food:

Games played:

Something disappointing:

Next time I'll do this differently:

Enchanted Rock State Natural Area
State: Texas   City: Fredericksburg   County: Gillespie

Plan your trip: https://tpwd.texas.gov/state-parks/enchanted-rock

Activities:

- ❑ Archery
- ❑ Biking
- ❑ Boating
- ❑ Campfire
- ❑ Caving
- ❑ Disc Golf
- ❑ Fishing
- ❑ Geo Cache
- ❑ Golf
- ❑ Hiking
- ❑ Horseback
- ❑ Hunting
- ❑ Jr. Ranger
- ❑ Park Tours
- ❑ Rock Climbing
- ❑ Stargazing
- ❑ Swimming
- ❑ Wildlife & Birding
- ❑
- ❑

Facilities:

- ❑ ADA
- ❑ Gym
- ❑ Historic Sites
- ❑ Lodge
- ❑ Meeting hall
- ❑ Pavilions
- ❑ Picnic sites
- ❑ Pool
- ❑ Restrooms
- ❑ Showers
- ❑ Visitor center
- ❑ RV Camp
- ❑ Tent Camp
- ❑ Yurt Camp
- ❑ Cabins
- ❑ Lodge rooms
- ❑ Group barracks
- ❑ Screened shelter

Notes:

____

____

____

____

____

____

____

____

Get the Facts

- ❑ Phone (830) 685-3636
- ❑ Park Hours

  ____

- ❑ Reservations? _____Y _____N

  date made_______________

- ❑ Open year 'round ___Y___N

  dates__________________

- ❑ Check in time ____________
- ❑ Check out time __________
- ❑ Dog friendly _____Y _____N
- ❑ Max RV length __________
- ❑ Distance from home

  miles: ________________

  hours: ________________

- ❑ Address________________

  ____

  ____

Fees:

- ❑ Day Use $ __________
- ❑ Camp Sites $ ________
- ❑ RV Sites $ __________
- ❑ Refund policy

  ____

  ____

  ____

Make It Personal

Trip dates: | The weather was:

Why I went:

How I got there: (circle all that apply)

I went with:

We stayed in (space, cabin # etc):

Most relaxing day:

Something funny:

Someone we met:

Best story told:

We liked this:

The best food:

Games played:

Something disappointing:

Next time I'll do this differently:

Fairfield Lake State Park

State: Texas   City: Fairfield   County: Freestone

Plan your trip: https://tpwd.texas.gov/state-parks/fairfield-lake

Activities:

- ❑ Archery
- ❑ Biking
- ❑ Boating
- ❑ Campfire
- ❑ Caving
- ❑ Disc Golf
- ❑ Fishing
- ❑ Geo Cache
- ❑ Golf
- ❑ Hiking
- ❑ Horseback
- ❑ Hunting
- ❑ Jr. Ranger
- ❑ Park Tours
- ❑ Rock Climbing
- ❑ Stargazing
- ❑ Swimming
- ❑ Wildlife & Birding
- ❑
- ❑

Facilities:

- ❑ ADA
- ❑ Gym
- ❑ Historic Sites
- ❑ Lodge
- ❑ Meeting hall
- ❑ Pavilions
- ❑ Picnic sites
- ❑ Pool
- ❑ Restrooms
- ❑ Showers
- ❑ Visitor center
- ❑ RV Camp
- ❑ Tent Camp
- ❑ Yurt Camp
- ❑ Cabins
- ❑ Lodge rooms
- ❑ Group barracks
- ❑ Screened shelter

Notes:

____

____

____

____

____

____

____

____

Get the Facts

- ❑ Phone (903) 389-4514
- ❑ Park Hours

____

- ❑ Reservations? _____Y _____N

date made________________

- ❑ Open year 'round ___Y___N

dates__________________

- ❑ Check in time ____________
- ❑ Check out time ____________
- ❑ Dog friendly ______Y ______N
- ❑ Max RV length ____________
- ❑ Distance from home

miles: __________________

hours: __________________

- ❑ Address________________

____

____

Fees:

- ❑ Day Use $ ____________
- ❑ Camp Sites $ __________
- ❑ RV Sites $ ___________
- ❑ Refund policy

____

____

Make It Personal

Trip dates: | The weather was:

Why I went:

How I got there: (circle all that apply)

I went with:

We stayed in (space, cabin # etc):

Most relaxing day:

Something funny:

Someone we met:

Best story told:

We liked this:

The best food:

Games played:

Something disappointing:

Next time I'll do this differently:

Falcon State Park

State: Texas   City: Falcon Heights   County: Starr

Plan your trip: https://tpwd.texas.gov/state-parks/falcon

Activities:

- ❑ Archery
- ❑ Biking
- ❑ Boating
- ❑ Campfire
- ❑ Caving
- ❑ Disc Golf
- ❑ Fishing
- ❑ Geo Cache
- ❑ Golf
- ❑ Hiking
- ❑ Horseback
- ❑ Hunting
- ❑ Jr. Ranger
- ❑ Park Tours
- ❑ Rock Climbing
- ❑ Stargazing
- ❑ Swimming
- ❑ Wildlife & Birding
- ❑
- ❑

Facilities:

- ❑ ADA
- ❑ Gym
- ❑ Historic Sites
- ❑ Lodge
- ❑ Meeting hall
- ❑ Pavilions
- ❑ Picnic sites
- ❑ Pool
- ❑ Restrooms
- ❑ Showers
- ❑ Visitor center
- ❑ RV Camp
- ❑ Tent Camp
- ❑ Yurt Camp
- ❑ Cabins
- ❑ Lodge rooms
- ❑ Group barracks
- ❑ Screened shelter

Notes:

____

____

____

____

____

____

____

____

____

____

____

Get the Facts

- ❑ Phone (956) 848-5327
- ❑ Park Hours

____

- ❑ Reservations? _____Y _____N

date made_______________

- ❑ Open year 'round ___Y___N

dates__________________

- ❑ Check in time ____________
- ❑ Check out time ___________
- ❑ Dog friendly _____Y _____N
- ❑ Max RV length ___________
- ❑ Distance from home

miles: _________________

hours: _________________

- ❑ Address________________

____

____

Fees:

- ❑ Day Use $ ___________
- ❑ Camp Sites $ _________
- ❑ RV Sites $ ___________
- ❑ Refund policy

____

____

____

Make It Personal

Trip dates: | The weather was:

Why I went:

How I got there: (circle all that apply)

I went with:

We stayed in (space, cabin # etc):

Most relaxing day:

Something funny:

Someone we met:

Best story told:

We liked this:

The best food:

Games played:

Something disappointing:

Next time I'll do this differently:

Fort Boggy State Park

State: Texas   **City: Centerville**   **County: Leon**

Plan your trip: https://tpwd.texas.gov/state-parks/fort-boggy

Activities:

- ❑ Archery
- ❑ Biking
- ❑ Boating
- ❑ Campfire
- ❑ Caving
- ❑ Disc Golf
- ❑ Fishing
- ❑ Geo Cache
- ❑ Golf
- ❑ Hiking
- ❑ Horseback
- ❑ Hunting
- ❑ Jr. Ranger
- ❑ Park Tours
- ❑ Rock Climbing
- ❑ Stargazing
- ❑ Swimming
- ❑ Wildlife & Birding
- ❑
- ❑

Facilities:

- ❑ ADA
- ❑ Gym
- ❑ Historic Sites
- ❑ Lodge
- ❑ Meeting hall
- ❑ Pavilions
- ❑ Picnic sites
- ❑ Pool
- ❑ Restrooms
- ❑ Showers
- ❑ Visitor center
- ❑ RV Camp
- ❑ Tent Camp
- ❑ Yurt Camp
- ❑ Cabins
- ❑ Lodge rooms
- ❑ Group barracks
- ❑ Screened shelter

Notes:

____

____

____

____

____

____

____

____

Get the Facts

- ❑ Phone (903) 344-1116
- ❑ Park Hours

  ____

- ❑ Reservations? ____Y ____N

  date made______________

- ❑ Open year 'round ___Y___N

  dates__________________

- ❑ Check in time ___________

- ❑ Check out time __________

- ❑ Dog friendly ______Y ______N

- ❑ Max RV length __________

- ❑ Distance from home

  miles: ________________

  hours: ________________

- ❑ Address________________

  ____

  ____

Fees:

- ❑ Day Use $ ___________
- ❑ Camp Sites $ _________
- ❑ RV Sites $ ___________
- ❑ Refund policy

  ____

  ____

  ____

Make It Personal

Trip dates: ___________________

The weather was:

Why I went: ___________________

How I got there: (circle all that apply)

I went with: ___________________

We stayed in (space, cabin # etc): ___________________

Most relaxing day: ___________________

Something funny: ___________________

Someone we met: ___________________

Best story told: ___________________

We liked this: ___________________

The best food: ___________________

Games played: ___________________

Something disappointing: ___________________

Next time I'll do this differently: ___________________

Fort Parker State Park

State: Texas   City: Mexia   County: Limestone

Plan your trip: https://tpwd.texas.gov/state-parks/fort-parker

Activities:

- ❑ Archery
- ❑ Biking
- ❑ Boating
- ❑ Campfire
- ❑ Caving
- ❑ Disc Golf
- ❑ Fishing
- ❑ Geo Cache
- ❑ Golf
- ❑ Hiking
- ❑ Horseback
- ❑ Hunting
- ❑ Jr. Ranger
- ❑ Park Tours
- ❑ Rock Climbing
- ❑ Stargazing
- ❑ Swimming
- ❑ Wildlife & Birding
- ❑
- ❑

Facilities:

- ❑ ADA
- ❑ Gym
- ❑ Historic Sites
- ❑ Lodge
- ❑ Meeting hall
- ❑ Pavilions
- ❑ Picnic sites
- ❑ Pool
- ❑ Restrooms
- ❑ Showers
- ❑ Visitor center
- ❑ RV Camp
- ❑ Tent Camp
- ❑ Yurt Camp
- ❑ Cabins
- ❑ Lodge rooms
- ❑ Group barracks
- ❑ Screened shelter

Notes:

____

____

____

____

____

____

____

____

Get the Facts

- ❑ Phone (254) 562-5751
- ❑ Park Hours

____

- ❑ Reservations? _____Y _____N

date made_______________

- ❑ Open year 'round ___Y___N

dates___________________

- ❑ Check in time ____________
- ❑ Check out time __________
- ❑ Dog friendly _____Y _____N
- ❑ Max RV length __________
- ❑ Distance from home

miles: _________________

hours: _________________

- ❑ Address________________

____

____

Fees:

- ❑ Day Use $ __________
- ❑ Camp Sites $ ________
- ❑ RV Sites $ __________
- ❑ Refund policy

____

____

____

Make It Personal

Trip dates: | The weather was:

Why I went:

How I got there: (circle all that apply)

I went with:

We stayed in (space, cabin # etc):

Most relaxing day:

Something funny:

Someone we met:

Best story told:

We liked this:

The best food:

Games played:

Something disappointing:

Next time I'll do this differently:

Fort Richardson State Park, Historic Site, Trailway
State: Texas   City: Jacksboro   County: Jack

Plan your trip: https://tpwd.texas.gov/state-parks/fort-richardson

Activities:

- ❑ Archery
- ❑ Biking
- ❑ Boating
- ❑ Campfire
- ❑ Caving
- ❑ Disc Golf
- ❑ Fishing
- ❑ Geo Cache
- ❑ Golf
- ❑ Hiking
- ❑ Horseback
- ❑ Hunting
- ❑ Jr. Ranger
- ❑ Park Tours
- ❑ Rock Climbing
- ❑ Stargazing
- ❑ Swimming
- ❑ Wildlife & Birding
- ❑
- ❑

Facilities:

- ❑ ADA
- ❑ Gym
- ❑ Historic Sites
- ❑ Lodge
- ❑ Meeting hall
- ❑ Pavilions
- ❑ Picnic sites
- ❑ Pool
- ❑ Restrooms
- ❑ Showers
- ❑ Visitor center
- ❑ RV Camp
- ❑ Tent Camp
- ❑ Yurt Camp
- ❑ Cabins
- ❑ Lodge rooms
- ❑ Group barracks
- ❑ Screened shelter

Notes:

____
____
____
____
____
____
____
____
____

Get the Facts

- ❑ Phone (940) 567-3506
- ❑ Park Hours

  ____

- ❑ Reservations? _____Y _____N

  date made______________

- ❑ Open year 'round ___Y___N

  dates__________________

- ❑ Check in time ____________
- ❑ Check out time ___________
- ❑ Dog friendly _____Y _____N
- ❑ Max RV length ___________
- ❑ Distance from home

  miles: _________________

  hours: _________________

- ❑ Address________________

  ____

  ____

Fees:

- ❑ Day Use $ ___________
- ❑ Camp Sites $ _________
- ❑ RV Sites $ ___________
- ❑ Refund policy

  ____

  ____

Make It Personal

Trip dates: | The weather was:

Why I went:

How I got there: (circle all that apply)

I went with:

We stayed in (space, cabin # etc):

Most relaxing day:

Something funny:

Someone we met:

Best story told:

We liked this:

The best food:

Games played:

Something disappointing:

Next time I'll do this differently:

Franklin Mountains State Park
State: Texas   City: El Paso   County: El Paso

Plan your trip: https://tpwd.texas.gov/state-parks/franklin-mountains

Activities:

- ❑ Archery
- ❑ Biking
- ❑ Boating
- ❑ Campfire
- ❑ Caving
- ❑ Disc Golf
- ❑ Fishing
- ❑ Geo Cache
- ❑ Golf
- ❑ Hiking
- ❑ Horseback
- ❑ Hunting
- ❑ Jr. Ranger
- ❑ Park Tours
- ❑ Rock Climbing
- ❑ Stargazing
- ❑ Swimming
- ❑ Wildlife & Birding
- ❑
- ❑

Facilities:

- ❑ ADA
- ❑ Gym
- ❑ Historic Sites
- ❑ Lodge
- ❑ Meeting hall
- ❑ Pavilions
- ❑ Picnic sites
- ❑ Pool
- ❑ Restrooms
- ❑ Showers
- ❑ Visitor center
- ❑ RV Camp
- ❑ Tent Camp
- ❑ Yurt Camp
- ❑ Cabins
- ❑ Lodge rooms
- ❑ Group barracks
- ❑ Screened shelter

Get the Facts

- ❑ Phone (915) 566-6441
- ❑ Park Hours

  ____

- ❑ Reservations? _____Y _____N

  date made_______________

- ❑ Open year 'round ___Y___N

  dates___________________

- ❑ Check in time ___________
- ❑ Check out time __________
- ❑ Dog friendly ______Y ______N
- ❑ Max RV length __________
- ❑ Distance from home

  miles: __________________

  hours: __________________

- ❑ Address________________

  ____

Fees:

- ❑ Day Use $ ___________
- ❑ Camp Sites $ _________
- ❑ RV Sites $ ___________
- ❑ Refund policy

  ____

  ____

Notes:

____

____

____

____

____

____

____

____

Make It Personal

Trip dates: | The weather was: 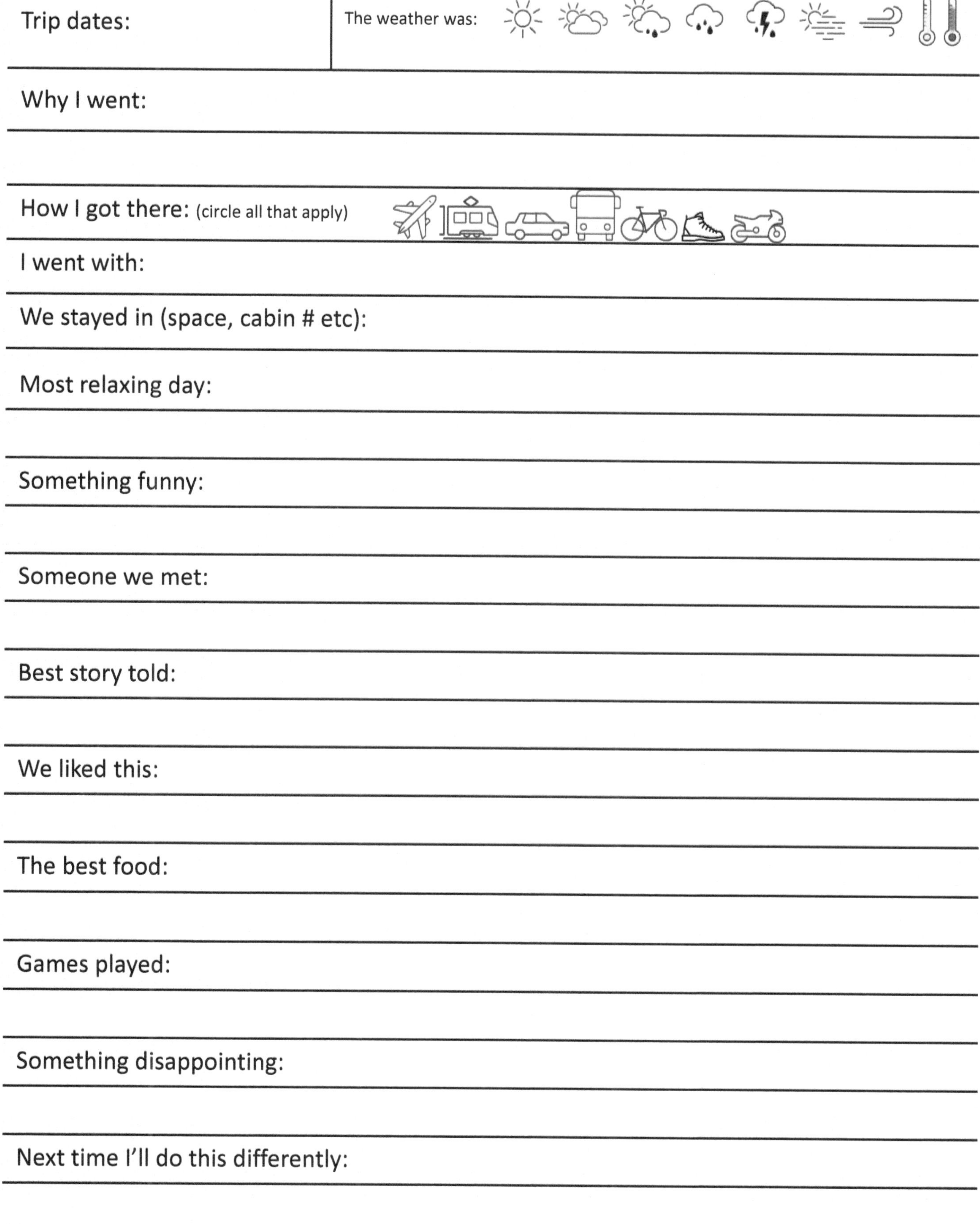

Why I went:

How I got there: (circle all that apply)

I went with:

We stayed in (space, cabin # etc):

Most relaxing day:

Something funny:

Someone we met:

Best story told:

We liked this:

The best food:

Games played:

Something disappointing:

Next time I'll do this differently:

Galveston Island State Park

State: Texas   **City: Galveston**   **County: Galveston**

Plan your trip: https://tpwd.texas.gov/state-parks/galveston-island

Activities:

- ❑ Archery
- ❑ Biking
- ❑ Boating
- ❑ Campfire
- ❑ Caving
- ❑ Disc Golf
- ❑ Fishing
- ❑ Geo Cache
- ❑ Golf
- ❑ Hiking
- ❑ Horseback
- ❑ Hunting
- ❑ Jr. Ranger
- ❑ Park Tours
- ❑ Rock Climbing
- ❑ Stargazing
- ❑ Swimming
- ❑ Wildlife & Birding
- ❑
- ❑

Facilities:

- ❑ ADA
- ❑ Gym
- ❑ Historic Sites
- ❑ Lodge
- ❑ Meeting hall
- ❑ Pavilions
- ❑ Picnic sites
- ❑ Pool
- ❑ Restrooms
- ❑ Showers
- ❑ Visitor center
- ❑ RV Camp
- ❑ Tent Camp
- ❑ Yurt Camp
- ❑ Cabins
- ❑ Lodge rooms
- ❑ Group barracks
- ❑ Screened shelter

Notes:

____

____

____

____

____

____

____

____

Get the Facts

- ❑ Phone (409) 737-1222
- ❑ Park Hours

    ____

- ❑ Reservations? _____Y _____N

    date made_______________

- ❑ Open year 'round ___Y___N

    dates__________________

- ❑ Check in time ___________

- ❑ Check out time __________

- ❑ Dog friendly _____Y _____N

- ❑ Max RV length __________

- ❑ Distance from home

    miles: _________________

    hours: _________________

- ❑ Address________________

    ____

    ____

Fees:

- ❑ Day Use $ ___________
- ❑ Camp Sites $ _________
- ❑ RV Sites $ ___________
- ❑ Refund policy

    ____

    ____

    ____

Make It Personal

Trip dates: | The weather was:

Why I went:

How I got there: (circle all that apply)

I went with:

We stayed in (space, cabin # etc):

Most relaxing day:

Something funny:

Someone we met:

Best story told:

We liked this:

The best food:

Games played:

Something disappointing:

Next time I'll do this differently:

Garner State Park
State: Texas   City: Concan   County: Uvalde

Plan your trip: https://tpwd.texas.gov/state-parks/garner

Activities:

- ❏ Archery
- ❏ Biking
- ❏ Boating
- ❏ Campfire
- ❏ Caving
- ❏ Disc Golf
- ❏ Fishing
- ❏ Geo Cache
- ❏ Golf
- ❏ Hiking
- ❏ Horseback
- ❏ Hunting
- ❏ Jr. Ranger
- ❏ Park Tours
- ❏ Rock Climbing
- ❏ Stargazing
- ❏ Swimming
- ❏ Wildlife & Birding
- ❏
- ❏

Facilities:

- ❏ ADA
- ❏ Gym
- ❏ Historic Sites
- ❏ Lodge
- ❏ Meeting hall
- ❏ Pavilions
- ❏ Picnic sites
- ❏ Pool
- ❏ Restrooms
- ❏ Showers
- ❏ Visitor center
- ❏ RV Camp
- ❏ Tent Camp
- ❏ Yurt Camp
- ❏ Cabins
- ❏ Lodge rooms
- ❏ Group barracks
- ❏ Screened shelter

Get the Facts

- ❏ Phone (830) 232-6132
- ❏ Park Hours

  ____

- ❏ Reservations? _____Y _____N

  date made_______________

- ❏ Open year 'round ___Y___N

  dates____________________

- ❏ Check in time ____________
- ❏ Check out time ___________
- ❏ Dog friendly ______Y ______N
- ❏ Max RV length ___________
- ❏ Distance from home

  miles: __________________

  hours: __________________

- ❏ Address________________

  ____

  ____

Fees:

- ❏ Day Use $ ___________
- ❏ Camp Sites $ _________
- ❏ RV Sites $ ___________
- ❏ Refund policy

  ____

  ____

  ____

Notes:

____

____

____

____

____

____

____

____

Make It Personal

Trip dates: | The weather was:

Why I went:

How I got there: (circle all that apply)

I went with:

We stayed in (space, cabin # etc):

Most relaxing day:

Something funny:

Someone we met:

Best story told:

We liked this:

The best food:

Games played:

Something disappointing:

Next time I'll do this differently:

Goliad State Park and Historic Site

State: Texas   City: Goliad   County: Goliad

Plan your trip: https://tpwd.texas.gov/state-parks/goliad

Activities:

- ❑ Archery
- ❑ Biking
- ❑ Boating
- ❑ Campfire
- ❑ Caving
- ❑ Disc Golf
- ❑ Fishing
- ❑ Geo Cache
- ❑ Golf
- ❑ Hiking
- ❑ Horseback
- ❑ Hunting
- ❑ Jr. Ranger
- ❑ Park Tours
- ❑ Rock Climbing
- ❑ Stargazing
- ❑ Swimming
- ❑ Wildlife & Birding
- ❑
- ❑

Facilities:

- ❑ ADA
- ❑ Gym
- ❑ Historic Sites
- ❑ Lodge
- ❑ Meeting hall
- ❑ Pavilions
- ❑ Picnic sites
- ❑ Pool
- ❑ Restrooms
- ❑ Showers
- ❑ Visitor center
- ❑ RV Camp
- ❑ Tent Camp
- ❑ Yurt Camp
- ❑ Cabins
- ❑ Lodge rooms
- ❑ Group barracks
- ❑ Screened shelter

Get the Facts

- ❑ Phone (361) 645-3405
- ❑ Park Hours

  ____

- ❑ Reservations? _____ Y _____ N

  date made________________

- ❑ Open year 'round ___ Y ___ N

  dates____________________

- ❑ Check in time ____________
- ❑ Check out time ___________
- ❑ Dog friendly _____ Y _____ N
- ❑ Max RV length ___________
- ❑ Distance from home

  miles: _________________

  hours: _________________

- ❑ Address________________

  ____

  ____

Fees:

- ❑ Day Use $ ____________
- ❑ Camp Sites $ _________
- ❑ RV Sites $ ___________
- ❑ Refund policy

  ____

  ____

  ____

Notes:

____

____

____

____

____

____

____

____

Make It Personal

Trip dates:

The weather was:

Why I went:

How I got there: (circle all that apply)

I went with:

We stayed in (space, cabin # etc):

Most relaxing day:

Something funny:

Someone we met:

Best story told:

We liked this:

The best food:

Games played:

Something disappointing:

Next time I'll do this differently:

Goose Island State Park

State: Texas   **City: Rockport**   **County: Aransas**

Plan your trip: https://tpwd.texas.gov/state-parks/goose-island

Activities:

- ❏ Archery
- ❏ Biking
- ❏ Boating
- ❏ Campfire
- ❏ Caving
- ❏ Disc Golf
- ❏ Fishing
- ❏ Geo Cache
- ❏ Golf
- ❏ Hiking
- ❏ Horseback
- ❏ Hunting
- ❏ Jr. Ranger
- ❏ Park Tours
- ❏ Rock Climbing
- ❏ Stargazing
- ❏ Swimming
- ❏ Wildlife & Birding
- ❏
- ❏

Facilities:

- ❏ ADA
- ❏ Gym
- ❏ Historic Sites
- ❏ Lodge
- ❏ Meeting hall
- ❏ Pavilions
- ❏ Picnic sites
- ❏ Pool
- ❏ Restrooms
- ❏ Showers
- ❏ Visitor center
- ❏ RV Camp
- ❏ Tent Camp
- ❏ Yurt Camp
- ❏ Cabins
- ❏ Lodge rooms
- ❏ Group barracks
- ❏ Screened shelter

Notes:

____

____

____

____

____

____

____

____

____

Get the Facts

- ❏ Phone (361) 729-2858
- ❏ Park Hours

  ____

- ❏ Reservations? _____Y _____N

  date made_______________
- ❏ Open year 'round ___Y___N

  dates___________________
- ❏ Check in time ___________
- ❏ Check out time __________
- ❏ Dog friendly _____Y _____N
- ❏ Max RV length __________
- ❏ Distance from home

  miles: _________________

  hours: _________________
- ❏ Address_______________

  ____

  ____

Fees:

- ❏ Day Use $ ___________
- ❏ Camp Sites $ _________
- ❏ RV Sites $ ___________
- ❏ Refund policy

  ____

  ____

  ____

Make It Personal

Trip dates: | The weather was:

Why I went:

How I got there: (circle all that apply)

I went with:

We stayed in (space, cabin # etc):

Most relaxing day:

Something funny:

Someone we met:

Best story told:

We liked this:

The best food:

Games played:

Something disappointing:

Next time I'll do this differently:

Government Canyon State Nat. Area
State: Texas   City: San Antonio   County: Bexar

Plan your trip: https://tpwd.texas.gov/state-parks/government-canyon

Activities:

- ❑ Archery
- ❑ Biking
- ❑ Boating
- ❑ Campfire
- ❑ Caving
- ❑ Disc Golf
- ❑ Fishing
- ❑ Geo Cache
- ❑ Golf
- ❑ Hiking
- ❑ Horseback
- ❑ Hunting
- ❑ Jr. Ranger
- ❑ Park Tours
- ❑ Rock Climbing
- ❑ Stargazing
- ❑ Swimming
- ❑ Wildlife & Birding
- ❑
- ❑

Facilities:

- ❑ ADA
- ❑ Gym
- ❑ Historic Sites
- ❑ Lodge
- ❑ Meeting hall
- ❑ Pavilions
- ❑ Picnic sites
- ❑ Pool
- ❑ Restrooms
- ❑ Showers
- ❑ Visitor center
- ❑ RV Camp
- ❑ Tent Camp
- ❑ Yurt Camp
- ❑ Cabins
- ❑ Lodge rooms
- ❑ Group barracks
- ❑ Screened shelter

Notes:

____
____
____
____
____
____
____
____
____

Get the Facts

- ❑ Phone (210) 688-9055
- ❑ Park Hours

____

- ❑ Reservations? _____Y _____N

date made_______________

- ❑ Open year 'round ___Y___N

dates___________________

- ❑ Check in time ___________
- ❑ Check out time __________
- ❑ Dog friendly _____Y _____N
- ❑ Max RV length ___________
- ❑ Distance from home

miles: _________________

hours: _________________

- ❑ Address________________

____

____

Fees:

- ❑ Day Use $ ___________
- ❑ Camp Sites $ _________
- ❑ RV Sites $ ___________
- ❑ Refund policy

____

____

____

Make It Personal

Trip dates: ___________________ | The weather was:

Why I went:
____
____

How I got there: (circle all that apply)

I went with:
____

We stayed in (space, cabin # etc):
____

Most relaxing day:
____
____

Something funny:
____
____

Someone we met:
____
____

Best story told:
____
____

We liked this:
____
____

The best food:
____
____

Games played:
____
____

Something disappointing:
____
____

Next time I'll do this differently:
____
____

Guadalupe River State Park

State: Texas   City: Spring Branch   County: Comal

Plan your trip: https://tpwd.texas.gov/state-parks/guadalupe-river

Activities:

- ❑ Archery
- ❑ Biking
- ❑ Boating
- ❑ Campfire
- ❑ Caving
- ❑ Disc Golf
- ❑ Fishing
- ❑ Geo Cache
- ❑ Golf
- ❑ Hiking
- ❑ Horseback
- ❑ Hunting
- ❑ Jr. Ranger
- ❑ Park Tours
- ❑ Rock Climbing
- ❑ Stargazing
- ❑ Swimming
- ❑ Wildlife & Birding
- ❑
- ❑

Facilities:

- ❑ ADA
- ❑ Gym
- ❑ Historic Sites
- ❑ Lodge
- ❑ Meeting hall
- ❑ Pavilions
- ❑ Picnic sites
- ❑ Pool
- ❑ Restrooms
- ❑ Showers
- ❑ Visitor center
- ❑ RV Camp
- ❑ Tent Camp
- ❑ Yurt Camp
- ❑ Cabins
- ❑ Lodge rooms
- ❑ Group barracks
- ❑ Screened shelter

Notes:

____

____

____

____

____

____

____

____

____

Get the Facts

- ❑ Phone (830) 438-2656
- ❑ Park Hours

____

- ❑ Reservations? _____Y _____N

  date made_______________

- ❑ Open year 'round ___Y___N

  dates___________________

- ❑ Check in time ___________
- ❑ Check out time __________
- ❑ Dog friendly _____Y _____N
- ❑ Max RV length __________
- ❑ Distance from home

  miles: _________________

  hours: _________________

- ❑ Address_______________

  ____

Fees:

- ❑ Day Use $ ___________
- ❑ Camp Sites $ _________
- ❑ RV Sites $ ___________
- ❑ Refund policy

  ____

  ____

  ____

Make It Personal

Trip dates: | The weather was:

Why I went:

How I got there: (circle all that apply)

I went with:

We stayed in (space, cabin # etc):

Most relaxing day:

Something funny:

Someone we met:

Best story told:

We liked this:

The best food:

Games played:

Something disappointing:

Next time I'll do this differently:

Hill Country State Natural Area

State: Texas **City: Bandera** **County: Bandera**

Plan your trip: https://tpwd.texas.gov/state-parks/hill-country

Activities:

- ❑ Archery
- ❑ Biking
- ❑ Boating
- ❑ Campfire
- ❑ Caving
- ❑ Disc Golf
- ❑ Fishing
- ❑ Geo Cache
- ❑ Golf
- ❑ Hiking
- ❑ Horseback
- ❑ Hunting
- ❑ Jr. Ranger
- ❑ Park Tours
- ❑ Rock Climbing
- ❑ Stargazing
- ❑ Swimming
- ❑ Wildlife & Birding
- ❑
- ❑

Facilities:

- ❑ ADA
- ❑ Gym
- ❑ Historic Sites
- ❑ Lodge
- ❑ Meeting hall
- ❑ Pavilions
- ❑ Picnic sites
- ❑ Pool
- ❑ Restrooms
- ❑ Showers
- ❑ Visitor center
- ❑ RV Camp
- ❑ Tent Camp
- ❑ Yurt Camp
- ❑ Cabins
- ❑ Lodge rooms
- ❑ Group barracks
- ❑ Screened shelter

Notes:

____

____

____

____

____

____

____

____

Get the Facts

- ❑ Phone (830) 796-4413
- ❑ Park Hours

  ____

- ❑ Reservations? _____Y _____N

  date made_______________

- ❑ Open year 'round ___Y___N

  dates___________________

- ❑ Check in time ___________

- ❑ Check out time __________

- ❑ Dog friendly ______Y ______N

- ❑ Max RV length ___________

- ❑ Distance from home

  miles: ________________

  hours: ________________

- ❑ Address________________

  ____

  ____

Fees:

- ❑ Day Use $ ___________
- ❑ Camp Sites $ _________
- ❑ RV Sites $ __________
- ❑ Refund policy

  ____

  ____

  ____

Make It Personal

Trip dates: | The weather was:

Why I went:

How I got there: (circle all that apply)

I went with:

We stayed in (space, cabin # etc):

Most relaxing day:

Something funny:

Someone we met:

Best story told:

We liked this:

The best food:

Games played:

Something disappointing:

Next time I'll do this differently:

Hueco Tanks State Park **& Historic Site**

State: Texas   City: El Paso   County: El Paso

Plan your trip: https://tpwd.texas.gov/state-parks/hueco-tanks

Activities:

- ❑ Archery
- ❑ Biking
- ❑ Boating
- ❑ Campfire
- ❑ Caving
- ❑ Disc Golf
- ❑ Fishing
- ❑ Geo Cache
- ❑ Golf
- ❑ Hiking
- ❑ Horseback
- ❑ Hunting
- ❑ Jr. Ranger
- ❑ Park Tours
- ❑ Rock Climbing
- ❑ Stargazing
- ❑ Swimming
- ❑ Wildlife & Birding
- ❑
- ❑

Facilities:

- ❑ ADA
- ❑ Gym
- ❑ Historic Sites
- ❑ Lodge
- ❑ Meeting hall
- ❑ Pavilions
- ❑ Picnic sites
- ❑ Pool
- ❑ Restrooms
- ❑ Showers
- ❑ Visitor center
- ❑ RV Camp
- ❑ Tent Camp
- ❑ Yurt Camp
- ❑ Cabins
- ❑ Lodge rooms
- ❑ Group barracks
- ❑ Screened shelter

Notes:

____

____

____

____

____

____

____

____

Get the Facts

- ❑ Phone (915) 857-1135
- ❑ Park Hours

____

- ❑ Reservations? _____Y _____N

date made_______________

- ❑ Open year 'round ___Y___N

dates__________________

- ❑ Check in time ___________
- ❑ Check out time __________
- ❑ Dog friendly _____Y _____N
- ❑ Max RV length __________
- ❑ Distance from home

miles: _________________

hours: _________________

- ❑ Address________________

____

____

Fees:

- ❑ Day Use $ ___________
- ❑ Camp Sites $ _________
- ❑ RV Sites $ ___________
- ❑ Refund policy

____

____

____

Make It Personal

Trip dates: _______________ | The weather was:

Why I went: _______________

How I got there: (circle all that apply)

I went with: _______________

We stayed in (space, cabin # etc): _______________

Most relaxing day: _______________

Something funny: _______________

Someone we met: _______________

Best story told: _______________

We liked this: _______________

The best food: _______________

Games played: _______________

Something disappointing: _______________

Next time I'll do this differently: _______________

Huntsville State Park

State: Texas   City: Huntsville   County: Walker

Plan your trip: https://tpwd.texas.gov/state-parks/huntsville

Activities:

- ❑ Archery
- ❑ Biking
- ❑ Boating
- ❑ Campfire
- ❑ Caving
- ❑ Disc Golf
- ❑ Fishing
- ❑ Geo Cache
- ❑ Golf
- ❑ Hiking
- ❑ Horseback
- ❑ Hunting
- ❑ Jr. Ranger
- ❑ Park Tours
- ❑ Rock Climbing
- ❑ Stargazing
- ❑ Swimming
- ❑ Wildlife & Birding
- ❑
- ❑

Facilities:

- ❑ ADA
- ❑ Gym
- ❑ Historic Sites
- ❑ Lodge
- ❑ Meeting hall
- ❑ Pavilions
- ❑ Picnic sites
- ❑ Pool
- ❑ Restrooms
- ❑ Showers
- ❑ Visitor center
- ❑ RV Camp
- ❑ Tent Camp
- ❑ Yurt Camp
- ❑ Cabins
- ❑ Lodge rooms
- ❑ Group barracks
- ❑ Screened shelter

Notes:

____

____

____

____

____

____

____

____

Get the Facts

- ❑ Phone (936) 295-5644
- ❑ Park Hours

  ____

- ❑ Reservations? ____Y ____N

  date made______________

- ❑ Open year 'round ___Y___N

  dates__________________

- ❑ Check in time ___________

- ❑ Check out time __________

- ❑ Dog friendly _____Y _____N

- ❑ Max RV length __________

- ❑ Distance from home

  miles: ________________

  hours: ________________

- ❑ Address________________

  ____

  ____

Fees:

- ❑ Day Use $ ___________
- ❑ Camp Sites $ _________
- ❑ RV Sites $ ___________
- ❑ Refund policy

  ____

  ____

  ____

Make It Personal

Trip dates: | The weather was:

Why I went:

How I got there: (circle all that apply)

I went with:

We stayed in (space, cabin # etc):

Most relaxing day:

Something funny:

Someone we met:

Best story told:

We liked this:

The best food:

Games played:

Something disappointing:

Next time I'll do this differently:

Inks Lake State Park

State: Texas   City: Burnet   County: Burnet

Plan your trip: https://tpwd.texas.gov/state-parks/inks-lake

Activities:

- ❑ Archery
- ❑ Biking
- ❑ Boating
- ❑ Campfire
- ❑ Caving
- ❑ Disc Golf
- ❑ Fishing
- ❑ Geo Cache
- ❑ Golf
- ❑ Hiking
- ❑ Horseback
- ❑ Hunting
- ❑ Jr. Ranger
- ❑ Park Tours
- ❑ Rock Climbing
- ❑ Stargazing
- ❑ Swimming
- ❑ Wildlife & Birding
- ❑
- ❑

Facilities:

- ❑ ADA
- ❑ Gym
- ❑ Historic Sites
- ❑ Lodge
- ❑ Meeting hall
- ❑ Pavilions
- ❑ Picnic sites
- ❑ Pool
- ❑ Restrooms
- ❑ Showers
- ❑ Visitor center
- ❑ RV Camp
- ❑ Tent Camp
- ❑ Yurt Camp
- ❑ Cabins
- ❑ Lodge rooms
- ❑ Group barracks
- ❑ Screened shelter

Notes:

____

____

____

____

____

____

____

____

____

Get the Facts

- ❑ Phone (512) 793-2223
- ❑ Park Hours

____

- ❑ Reservations? _____Y _____N

date made_______________

- ❑ Open year 'round ___Y___N

dates___________________

- ❑ Check in time ____________
- ❑ Check out time ___________
- ❑ Dog friendly ______Y ______N
- ❑ Max RV length ___________
- ❑ Distance from home

miles: _________________

hours: _________________

- ❑ Address________________

____

____

Fees:

- ❑ Day Use $ ___________
- ❑ Camp Sites $ _________
- ❑ RV Sites $ ___________
- ❑ Refund policy

____

____

____

Make It Personal

Trip dates: ___________________ | The weather was:

____

Why I went:

____

How I got there: (circle all that apply)

____

I went with:

____

We stayed in (space, cabin # etc):

____

Most relaxing day:

____

Something funny:

____

Someone we met:

____

Best story told:

____

We liked this:

____

The best food:

____

Games played:

____

Something disappointing:

____

Next time I'll do this differently:

____

Kickapoo Cavern State Park
State: Texas　　　City: Brackettville　　County: Kinney

Plan your trip: https://tpwd.texas.gov/state-parks/kickapoo-cavern

Activities:

- ❑ Archery
- ❑ Biking
- ❑ Boating
- ❑ Campfire
- ❑ Caving
- ❑ Disc Golf
- ❑ Fishing
- ❑ Geo Cache
- ❑ Golf
- ❑ Hiking
- ❑ Horseback
- ❑ Hunting
- ❑ Jr. Ranger
- ❑ Park Tours
- ❑ Rock Climbing
- ❑ Stargazing
- ❑ Swimming
- ❑ Wildlife & Birding
- ❑
- ❑

Facilities:

- ❑ ADA
- ❑ Gym
- ❑ Historic Sites
- ❑ Lodge
- ❑ Meeting hall
- ❑ Pavilions
- ❑ Picnic sites
- ❑ Pool
- ❑ Restrooms
- ❑ Showers
- ❑ Visitor center
- ❑ RV Camp
- ❑ Tent Camp
- ❑ Yurt Camp
- ❑ Cabins
- ❑ Lodge rooms
- ❑ Group barracks
- ❑ Screened shelter

Notes:

____

____

____

____

____

____

____

____

____

Get the Facts

- ❑ Phone (830) 563-2342
- ❑ Park Hours

____

- ❑ Reservations? _____Y _____N

date made_______________

- ❑ Open year 'round ___Y___N

dates__________________________

- ❑ Check in time _____________
- ❑ Check out time ____________
- ❑ Dog friendly ______Y ______N
- ❑ Max RV length ____________
- ❑ Distance from home

miles: ___________________

hours: ___________________

- ❑ Address__________________

____

____

Fees:

- ❑ Day Use $ ____________
- ❑ Camp Sites $ __________
- ❑ RV Sites $ ____________
- ❑ Refund policy

____

____

Make It Personal

Trip dates: | The weather was:

Why I went:

How I got there: (circle all that apply)

I went with:

We stayed in (space, cabin # etc):

Most relaxing day:

Something funny:

Someone we met:

Best story told:

We liked this:

The best food:

Games played:

Something disappointing:

Next time I'll do this differently:

Lake Arrowhead State Park
State: Texas   City: Wichita Falls   County: Wichita

Plan your trip: https://tpwd.texas.gov/state-parks/lake-arrowhead

Activities:

- ❑ Archery
- ❑ Biking
- ❑ Boating
- ❑ Campfire
- ❑ Caving
- ❑ Disc Golf
- ❑ Fishing
- ❑ Geo Cache
- ❑ Golf
- ❑ Hiking
- ❑ Horseback
- ❑ Hunting
- ❑ Jr. Ranger
- ❑ Park Tours
- ❑ Rock Climbing
- ❑ Stargazing
- ❑ Swimming
- ❑ Wildlife & Birding
- ❑
- ❑

Facilities:

- ❑ ADA
- ❑ Gym
- ❑ Historic Sites
- ❑ Lodge
- ❑ Meeting hall
- ❑ Pavilions
- ❑ Picnic sites
- ❑ Pool
- ❑ Restrooms
- ❑ Showers
- ❑ Visitor center
- ❑ RV Camp
- ❑ Tent Camp
- ❑ Yurt Camp
- ❑ Cabins
- ❑ Lodge rooms
- ❑ Group barracks
- ❑ Screened shelter

Notes:

____

____

____

____

____

____

____

____

Get the Facts

- ❑ Phone (940) 528-2211
- ❑ Park Hours

____

- ❑ Reservations? _____Y _____N

  date made_______________

- ❑ Open year 'round ___Y___N

  dates__________________

- ❑ Check in time ___________

- ❑ Check out time __________

- ❑ Dog friendly _____Y _____N

- ❑ Max RV length __________

- ❑ Distance from home

  miles: ________________

  hours: ________________

- ❑ Address________________

____

____

Fees:

- ❑ Day Use $ ___________
- ❑ Camp Sites $ _________
- ❑ RV Sites $ __________
- ❑ Refund policy

____

____

____

Make It Personal

Trip dates: | The weather was:

Why I went:

How I got there: (circle all that apply)

I went with:

We stayed in (space, cabin # etc):

Most relaxing day:

Something funny:

Someone we met:

Best story told:

We liked this:

The best food:

Games played:

Something disappointing:

Next time I'll do this differently:

Lake Bob Sandlin State Park
State: Texas   City: Pittsburg   County: Camp

Plan your trip: https://tpwd.texas.gov/state-parks/lake-bob-sandlin

Activities:

- ❏ Archery
- ❏ Biking
- ❏ Boating
- ❏ Campfire
- ❏ Caving
- ❏ Disc Golf
- ❏ Fishing
- ❏ Geo Cache
- ❏ Golf
- ❏ Hiking
- ❏ Horseback
- ❏ Hunting
- ❏ Jr. Ranger
- ❏ Park Tours
- ❏ Rock Climbing
- ❏ Stargazing
- ❏ Swimming
- ❏ Wildlife & Birding
- ❏
- ❏

Facilities:

- ❏ ADA
- ❏ Gym
- ❏ Historic Sites
- ❏ Lodge
- ❏ Meeting hall
- ❏ Pavilions
- ❏ Picnic sites
- ❏ Pool
- ❏ Restrooms
- ❏ Showers
- ❏ Visitor center
- ❏ RV Camp
- ❏ Tent Camp
- ❏ Yurt Camp
- ❏ Cabins
- ❏ Lodge rooms
- ❏ Group barracks
- ❏ Screened shelter

Notes:

____

____

____

____

____

____

____

____

Get the Facts

- ❏ Phone (903) 572-5531
- ❏ Park Hours

____

- ❏ Reservations? _____Y _____N

date made_______________

- ❏ Open year 'round ___Y___N

dates___________________

- ❏ Check in time ____________
- ❏ Check out time ___________
- ❏ Dog friendly _____Y _____N
- ❏ Max RV length ___________
- ❏ Distance from home

miles: __________________

hours: __________________

- ❏ Address________________

____

____

Fees:

- ❏ Day Use $ ___________
- ❏ Camp Sites $ _________
- ❏ RV Sites $ ___________
- ❏ Refund policy

____

____

____

Make It Personal

Trip dates: | The weather was:

Why I went:

How I got there: (circle all that apply)

I went with:

We stayed in (space, cabin # etc):

Most relaxing day:

Something funny:

Someone we met:

Best story told:

We liked this:

The best food:

Games played:

Something disappointing:

Next time I'll do this differently:

Lake Brownwood State Park
State: Texas   City: Lake Brownwood   County: Brown

Plan your trip: https://tpwd.texas.gov/state-parks/lake-brownwood

Activities:

- Archery
- Biking
- Boating
- Campfire
- Caving
- Disc Golf
- Fishing
- Geo Cache
- Golf
- Hiking
- Horseback
- Hunting
- Jr. Ranger
- Park Tours
- Rock Climbing
- Stargazing
- Swimming
- Wildlife & Birding
-
-

Facilities:

- ADA
- Gym
- Historic Sites
- Lodge
- Meeting hall
- Pavilions
- Picnic sites
- Pool
- Restrooms
- Showers
- Visitor center
- RV Camp
- Tent Camp
- Yurt Camp
- Cabins
- Lodge rooms
- Group barracks
- Screened shelter

Notes:

____

____

____

____

____

____

____

____

Get the Facts

- Phone (325) 784-5223
- Park Hours

  ____

- Reservations? ____Y ____N

  date made______________

- Open year 'round ___Y___N

  dates__________________

- Check in time ___________

- Check out time __________

- Dog friendly _____Y _____N

- Max RV length __________

- Distance from home

  miles: ________________

  hours: ________________

- Address________________

  ____

  ____

Fees:

- Day Use $ __________
- Camp Sites $ _________
- RV Sites $ __________
- Refund policy

  ____

  ____

  ____

Make It Personal

Trip dates: | The weather was:

Why I went:

How I got there: (circle all that apply)

I went with:

We stayed in (space, cabin # etc):

Most relaxing day:

Something funny:

Someone we met:

Best story told:

We liked this:

The best food:

Games played:

Something disappointing:

Next time I'll do this differently:

Lake Casa Blanca Int'l State Park
State: Texas   City: Laredo   County: Webb

Plan your trip: https://tpwd.texas.gov/state-parks/lake-casa-blanca

Activities:

- ❑ Archery
- ❑ Biking
- ❑ Boating
- ❑ Campfire
- ❑ Caving
- ❑ Disc Golf
- ❑ Fishing
- ❑ Geo Cache
- ❑ Golf
- ❑ Hiking
- ❑ Horseback
- ❑ Hunting
- ❑ Jr. Ranger
- ❑ Park Tours
- ❑ Rock Climbing
- ❑ Stargazing
- ❑ Swimming
- ❑ Wildlife & Birding
- ❑
- ❑

Facilities:

- ❑ ADA
- ❑ Gym
- ❑ Historic Sites
- ❑ Lodge
- ❑ Meeting hall
- ❑ Pavilions
- ❑ Picnic sites
- ❑ Pool
- ❑ Restrooms
- ❑ Showers
- ❑ Visitor center
- ❑ RV Camp
- ❑ Tent Camp
- ❑ Yurt Camp
- ❑ Cabins
- ❑ Lodge rooms
- ❑ Group barracks
- ❑ Screened shelter

Notes:

____

____

____

____

____

____

____

____

Get the Facts

- ❑ Phone (956) 725-3826
- ❑ Park Hours

____

- ❑ Reservations? _____Y _____N

date made_______________

- ❑ Open year 'round ___Y___N

dates__________________

- ❑ Check in time ____________
- ❑ Check out time ___________
- ❑ Dog friendly ______Y ______N
- ❑ Max RV length ___________
- ❑ Distance from home

miles: ____________________

hours: ____________________

- ❑ Address________________

____

____

Fees:

- ❑ Day Use $ ____________
- ❑ Camp Sites $ __________
- ❑ RV Sites $ ___________
- ❑ Refund policy

____

____

Make It Personal

Trip dates: | The weather was:

Why I went:

How I got there: (circle all that apply)

I went with:

We stayed in (space, cabin # etc):

Most relaxing day:

Something funny:

Someone we met:

Best story told:

We liked this:

The best food:

Games played:

Something disappointing:

Next time I'll do this differently:

Lake Colorado City State Park

State: Texas   City: Colorado City   County: Mitchell

Plan your trip: https://tpwd.texas.gov/state-parks/lake-colorado-city

Activities:

- ❏ Archery
- ❏ Biking
- ❏ Boating
- ❏ Campfire
- ❏ Caving
- ❏ Disc Golf
- ❏ Fishing
- ❏ Geo Cache
- ❏ Golf
- ❏ Hiking
- ❏ Horseback
- ❏ Hunting
- ❏ Jr. Ranger
- ❏ Park Tours
- ❏ Rock Climbing
- ❏ Stargazing
- ❏ Swimming
- ❏ Wildlife & Birding
- ❏
- ❏

Facilities:

- ❏ ADA
- ❏ Gym
- ❏ Historic Sites
- ❏ Lodge
- ❏ Meeting hall
- ❏ Pavilions
- ❏ Picnic sites
- ❏ Pool
- ❏ Restrooms
- ❏ Showers
- ❏ Visitor center
- ❏ RV Camp
- ❏ Tent Camp
- ❏ Yurt Camp
- ❏ Cabins
- ❏ Lodge rooms
- ❏ Group barracks
- ❏ Screened shelter

Notes:

____

____

____

____

____

____

____

____

Get the Facts

- ❏ Phone (325) 728-3931
- ❏ Park Hours

____

- ❏ Reservations? _____Y _____N

date made_______________

- ❏ Open year 'round ___Y___N

dates__________________

- ❏ Check in time ___________
- ❏ Check out time __________
- ❏ Dog friendly _____Y _____N
- ❏ Max RV length __________
- ❏ Distance from home

miles: ________________

hours: ________________

- ❏ Address________________

____

____

Fees:

- ❏ Day Use $ __________
- ❏ Camp Sites $ _________
- ❏ RV Sites $ __________
- ❏ Refund policy

____

____

____

Make It Personal

Trip dates:

The weather was:

Why I went:

How I got there: (circle all that apply)

I went with:

We stayed in (space, cabin # etc):

Most relaxing day:

Something funny:

Someone we met:

Best story told:

We liked this:

The best food:

Games played:

Something disappointing:

Next time I'll do this differently:

Lake Corpus Christi State Park

State: Texas   City: Mathis   County: San Patricio

Plan your trip: https://tpwd.texas.gov/state-parks/lake-corpus-christi

Activities:

- ❑ Archery
- ❑ Biking
- ❑ Boating
- ❑ Campfire
- ❑ Caving
- ❑ Disc Golf
- ❑ Fishing
- ❑ Geo Cache
- ❑ Golf
- ❑ Hiking
- ❑ Horseback
- ❑ Hunting
- ❑ Jr. Ranger
- ❑ Park Tours
- ❑ Rock Climbing
- ❑ Stargazing
- ❑ Swimming
- ❑ Wildlife & Birding
- ❑
- ❑

Facilities:

- ❑ ADA
- ❑ Gym
- ❑ Historic Sites
- ❑ Lodge
- ❑ Meeting hall
- ❑ Pavilions
- ❑ Picnic sites
- ❑ Pool
- ❑ Restrooms
- ❑ Showers
- ❑ Visitor center
- ❑ RV Camp
- ❑ Tent Camp
- ❑ Yurt Camp
- ❑ Cabins
- ❑ Lodge rooms
- ❑ Group barracks
- ❑ Screened shelter

Notes:

____

____

____

____

____

____

____

____

Get the Facts

- ❑ Phone (361) 547-2635
- ❑ Park Hours

  ____

- ❑ Reservations? _____Y _____N

  date made______________
- ❑ Open year 'round ___Y___N

  dates__________________
- ❑ Check in time ___________
- ❑ Check out time __________
- ❑ Dog friendly ______Y _____N
- ❑ Max RV length __________
- ❑ Distance from home

  miles: __________________

  hours: __________________
- ❑ Address________________

  ____

  ____

Fees:

- ❑ Day Use $ ___________
- ❑ Camp Sites $ _________
- ❑ RV Sites $ ___________
- ❑ Refund policy

  ____

  ____

Make It Personal

Trip dates: | The weather was:

Why I went:

How I got there: (circle all that apply)

I went with:

We stayed in (space, cabin # etc):

Most relaxing day:

Something funny:

Someone we met:

Best story told:

We liked this:

The best food:

Games played:

Something disappointing:

Next time I'll do this differently:

Lake Livingston State Park

State: Texas   City: Livingston   County: Polk

Plan your trip: https://tpwd.texas.gov/state-parks/lake-livingston

Activities:

- ❏ Archery
- ❏ Biking
- ❏ Boating
- ❏ Campfire
- ❏ Caving
- ❏ Disc Golf
- ❏ Fishing
- ❏ Geo Cache
- ❏ Golf
- ❏ Hiking
- ❏ Horseback
- ❏ Hunting
- ❏ Jr. Ranger
- ❏ Park Tours
- ❏ Rock Climbing
- ❏ Stargazing
- ❏ Swimming
- ❏ Wildlife & Birding
- ❏
- ❏

Facilities:

- ❏ ADA
- ❏ Gym
- ❏ Historic Sites
- ❏ Lodge
- ❏ Meeting hall
- ❏ Pavilions
- ❏ Picnic sites
- ❏ Pool
- ❏ Restrooms
- ❏ Showers
- ❏ Visitor center
- ❏ RV Camp
- ❏ Tent Camp
- ❏ Yurt Camp
- ❏ Cabins
- ❏ Lodge rooms
- ❏ Group barracks
- ❏ Screened shelter

Get the Facts

- ❏ Phone (936) 365-2201
- ❏ Park Hours

  ____

- ❏ Reservations? ____Y ____N

  date made_______________

- ❏ Open year 'round ___Y___N

  dates__________________

- ❏ Check in time ___________
- ❏ Check out time __________
- ❏ Dog friendly _____Y _____N
- ❏ Max RV length __________
- ❏ Distance from home

  miles: ________________

  hours: ________________

- ❏ Address_______________

  ____

Fees:

- ❏ Day Use $ __________
- ❏ Camp Sites $ ________
- ❏ RV Sites $ __________
- ❏ Refund policy

  ____

  ____

  ____

Notes:

____

____

____

____

____

____

____

____

Make It Personal

Trip dates: | The weather was:

Why I went:

How I got there: (circle all that apply)

I went with:

We stayed in (space, cabin # etc):

Most relaxing day:

Something funny:

Someone we met:

Best story told:

We liked this:

The best food:

Games played:

Something disappointing:

Next time I'll do this differently:

Lake Mineral Wells State Park & Trailway

State: Texas   City: Mineral Wells   County: Parker

Plan your trip: https://tpwd.texas.gov/state-parks/lake-mineral-wells

Activities:

- ❑ Archery
- ❑ Biking
- ❑ Boating
- ❑ Campfire
- ❑ Caving
- ❑ Disc Golf
- ❑ Fishing
- ❑ Geo Cache
- ❑ Golf
- ❑ Hiking
- ❑ Horseback
- ❑ Hunting
- ❑ Jr. Ranger
- ❑ Park Tours
- ❑ Rock Climbing
- ❑ Stargazing
- ❑ Swimming
- ❑ Wildlife & Birding
- ❑
- ❑

Facilities:

- ❑ ADA
- ❑ Gym
- ❑ Historic Sites
- ❑ Lodge
- ❑ Meeting hall
- ❑ Pavilions
- ❑ Picnic sites
- ❑ Pool
- ❑ Restrooms
- ❑ Showers
- ❑ Visitor center
- ❑ RV Camp
- ❑ Tent Camp
- ❑ Yurt Camp
- ❑ Cabins
- ❑ Lodge rooms
- ❑ Group barracks
- ❑ Screened shelter

Notes:

____

____

____

____

____

____

____

____

Get the Facts

- ❑ Phone (940) 328-1171
- ❑ Park Hours

  ____

- ❑ Reservations? _____Y _____N

  date made_______________

- ❑ Open year 'round ___Y___N

  dates___________________

- ❑ Check in time ___________

- ❑ Check out time __________

- ❑ Dog friendly ______Y ______N

- ❑ Max RV length __________

- ❑ Distance from home

  miles: ________________

  hours: ________________

- ❑ Address_______________

  ____

  ____

Fees:

- ❑ Day Use $ ___________
- ❑ Camp Sites $ _________
- ❑ RV Sites $ ___________
- ❑ Refund policy

  ____

  ____

Make It Personal

Trip dates: | The weather was:

Why I went:

How I got there: (circle all that apply)

I went with:

We stayed in (space, cabin # etc):

Most relaxing day:

Something funny:

Someone we met:

Best story told:

We liked this:

The best food:

Games played:

Something disappointing:

Next time I'll do this differently:

Lake Somerville State Park-Birch Creek

State: Texas   City: Somerville   County: Burleson

Plan your trip: https://tpwd.texas.gov/state-parks/lake-somerville

Activities:

- ❏ Archery
- ❏ Biking
- ❏ Boating
- ❏ Campfire
- ❏ Caving
- ❏ Disc Golf
- ❏ Fishing
- ❏ Geo Cache
- ❏ Golf
- ❏ Hiking
- ❏ Horseback
- ❏ Hunting
- ❏ Jr. Ranger
- ❏ Park Tours
- ❏ Rock Climbing
- ❏ Stargazing
- ❏ Swimming
- ❏ Wildlife & Birding
- ❏
- ❏

Facilities:

- ❏ ADA
- ❏ Gym
- ❏ Historic Sites
- ❏ Lodge
- ❏ Meeting hall
- ❏ Pavilions
- ❏ Picnic sites
- ❏ Pool
- ❏ Restrooms
- ❏ Showers
- ❏ Visitor center
- ❏ RV Camp
- ❏ Tent Camp
- ❏ Yurt Camp
- ❏ Cabins
- ❏ Lodge rooms
- ❏ Group barracks
- ❏ Screened shelter

Get the Facts

- ❏ Phone (979) 535-7763
- ❏ Park Hours

  ____

- ❏ Reservations? _____Y _____N

  date made_______________
- ❏ Open year 'round ___Y___N

  dates___________________
- ❏ Check in time ___________
- ❏ Check out time __________
- ❏ Dog friendly _____Y _____N
- ❏ Max RV length __________
- ❏ Distance from home

  miles: _________________

  hours: _________________
- ❏ Address________________

  ____

Notes:

____

____

____

____

____

____

____

____

Fees:

- ❏ Day Use $ __________
- ❏ Camp Sites $ ________
- ❏ RV Sites $ __________
- ❏ Refund policy

  ____

  ____

  ____

Make It Personal

Trip dates: The weather was: 

Why I went:

How I got there: (circle all that apply)

I went with:

We stayed in (space, cabin # etc):

Most relaxing day:

Something funny:

Someone we met:

Best story told:

We liked this:

The best food:

Games played:

Something disappointing:

Next time I'll do this differently:

Lake Somerville State Park-Nails Creek

State: Texas   **City: Ledbetter**   **County: Fayette**

Plan your trip: https://tpwd.texas.gov/state-parks/lake-somerville

Activities:

- ❑ Archery
- ❑ Biking
- ❑ Boating
- ❑ Campfire
- ❑ Caving
- ❑ Disc Golf
- ❑ Fishing
- ❑ Geo Cache
- ❑ Golf
- ❑ Hiking
- ❑ Horseback
- ❑ Hunting
- ❑ Jr. Ranger
- ❑ Park Tours
- ❑ Rock Climbing
- ❑ Stargazing
- ❑ Swimming
- ❑ Wildlife & Birding
- ❑
- ❑

Facilities:

- ❑ ADA
- ❑ Gym
- ❑ Historic Sites
- ❑ Lodge
- ❑ Meeting hall
- ❑ Pavilions
- ❑ Picnic sites
- ❑ Pool
- ❑ Restrooms
- ❑ Showers
- ❑ Visitor center
- ❑ RV Camp
- ❑ Tent Camp
- ❑ Yurt Camp
- ❑ Cabins
- ❑ Lodge rooms
- ❑ Group barracks
- ❑ Screened shelter

Notes:

____
____
____
____
____
____
____
____
____

Get the Facts

- ❑ Phone (979) 289-2392
- ❑ Park Hours

  ____

- ❑ Reservations? _____Y _____N

  date made_______________
- ❑ Open year 'round ___Y___N

  dates___________________
- ❑ Check in time ____________
- ❑ Check out time ___________
- ❑ Dog friendly ______Y ______N
- ❑ Max RV length ___________
- ❑ Distance from home

  miles: __________________

  hours: __________________
- ❑ Address________________

  ____

  ____

Fees:

- ❑ Day Use $ ____________
- ❑ Camp Sites $ __________
- ❑ RV Sites $ ___________
- ❑ Refund policy

  ____

  ____

Make It Personal

Trip dates: | The weather was:

Why I went:

How I got there: (circle all that apply)

I went with:

We stayed in (space, cabin # etc):

Most relaxing day:

Something funny:

Someone we met:

Best story told:

We liked this:

The best food:

Games played:

Something disappointing:

Next time I'll do this differently:

Lake Tawakoni State Park

State: Texas   City: Wills Point   County: Van Zandt

Plan your trip: https://tpwd.texas.gov/state-parks/lake-tawakoni

Activities:

- ❏ Archery
- ❏ Biking
- ❏ Boating
- ❏ Campfire
- ❏ Caving
- ❏ Disc Golf
- ❏ Fishing
- ❏ Geo Cache
- ❏ Golf
- ❏ Hiking
- ❏ Horseback
- ❏ Hunting
- ❏ Jr. Ranger
- ❏ Park Tours
- ❏ Rock Climbing
- ❏ Stargazing
- ❏ Swimming
- ❏ Wildlife & Birding
- ❏
- ❏

Facilities:

- ❏ ADA
- ❏ Gym
- ❏ Historic Sites
- ❏ Lodge
- ❏ Meeting hall
- ❏ Pavilions
- ❏ Picnic sites
- ❏ Pool
- ❏ Restrooms
- ❏ Showers
- ❏ Visitor center
- ❏ RV Camp
- ❏ Tent Camp
- ❏ Yurt Camp
- ❏ Cabins
- ❏ Lodge rooms
- ❏ Group barracks
- ❏ Screened shelter

Notes:

____

____

____

____

____

____

____

____

Get the Facts

- ❏ Phone (903) 560-7123
- ❏ Park Hours

  ____

- ❏ Reservations? _____Y _____N

  date made_______________

- ❏ Open year 'round ___Y___N

  dates__________________

- ❏ Check in time ___________

- ❏ Check out time __________

- ❏ Dog friendly _____Y _____N

- ❏ Max RV length __________

- ❏ Distance from home

  miles: _________________

  hours: _________________

- ❏ Address________________

  ____

  ____

Fees:

- ❏ Day Use $ ___________
- ❏ Camp Sites $ _________
- ❏ RV Sites $ ___________
- ❏ Refund policy

  ____

  ____

  ____

Make It Personal

Trip dates: | The weather was:

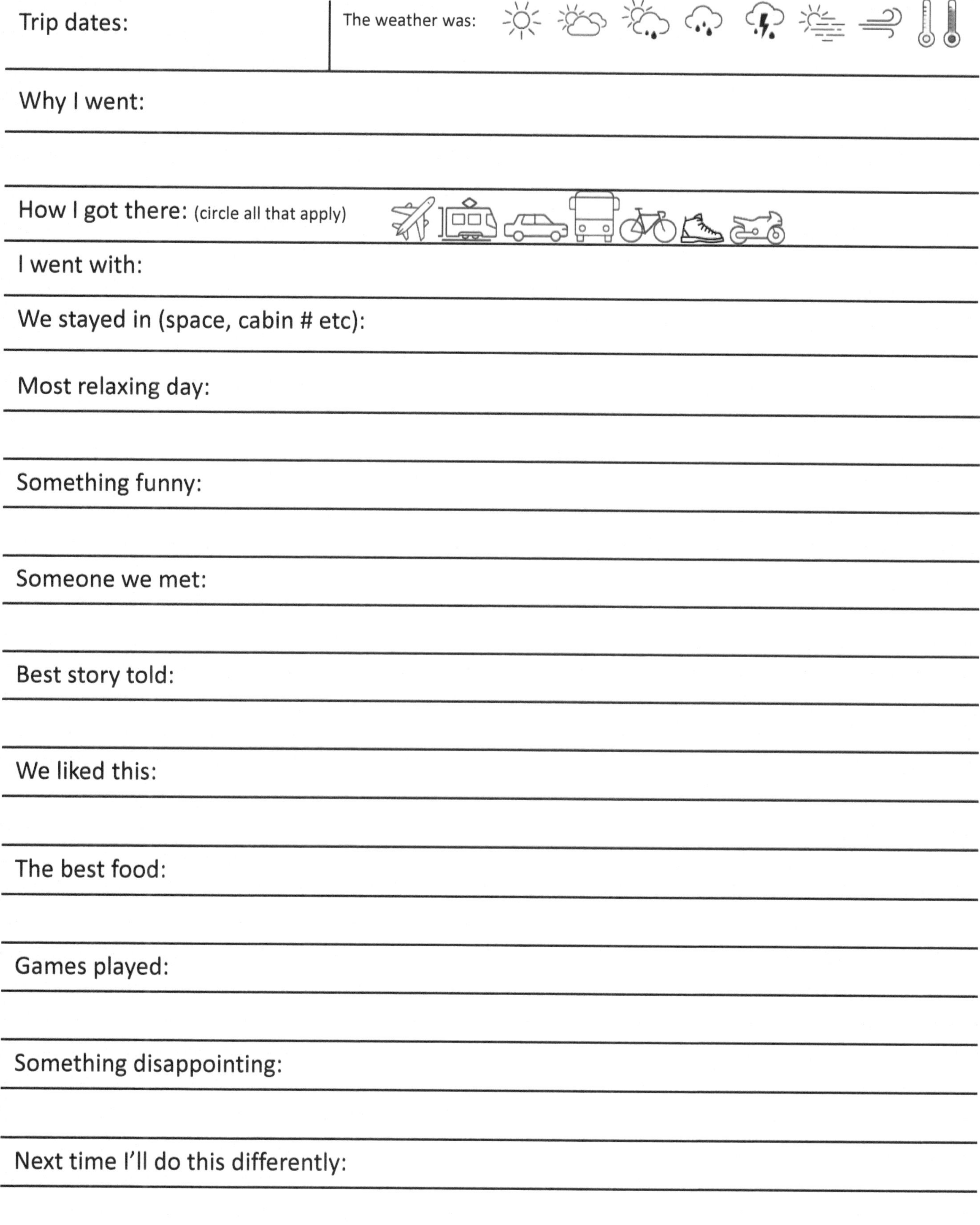

Why I went:

How I got there: (circle all that apply)

I went with:

We stayed in (space, cabin # etc):

Most relaxing day:

Something funny:

Someone we met:

Best story told:

We liked this:

The best food:

Games played:

Something disappointing:

Next time I'll do this differently:

Lake Whitney State Park
State: Texas   City: Whitney   County: Hill

Plan your trip: https://tpwd.texas.gov/state-parks/lake-whitney

Activities:

- ❏ Archery
- ❏ Biking
- ❏ Boating
- ❏ Campfire
- ❏ Caving
- ❏ Disc Golf
- ❏ Fishing
- ❏ Geo Cache
- ❏ Golf
- ❏ Hiking
- ❏ Horseback
- ❏ Hunting
- ❏ Jr. Ranger
- ❏ Park Tours
- ❏ Rock Climbing
- ❏ Stargazing
- ❏ Swimming
- ❏ Wildlife & Birding
- ❏
- ❏

Facilities:

- ❏ ADA
- ❏ Gym
- ❏ Historic Sites
- ❏ Lodge
- ❏ Meeting hall
- ❏ Pavilions
- ❏ Picnic sites
- ❏ Pool
- ❏ Restrooms
- ❏ Showers
- ❏ Visitor center
- ❏ RV Camp
- ❏ Tent Camp
- ❏ Yurt Camp
- ❏ Cabins
- ❏ Lodge rooms
- ❏ Group barracks
- ❏ Screened shelter

Notes:

____

____

____

____

____

____

____

____

____

Get the Facts

- ❏ Phone (254) 694-3793
- ❏ Park Hours

____

- ❏ Reservations? _____Y _____N

date made_______________

- ❏ Open year 'round ___Y___N

dates_____________________

- ❏ Check in time ____________
- ❏ Check out time __________
- ❏ Dog friendly ______Y ______N
- ❏ Max RV length __________
- ❏ Distance from home

miles: ___________________

hours: ___________________

- ❏ Address_________________

____

____

Fees:

- ❏ Day Use $ ___________
- ❏ Camp Sites $ _________
- ❏ RV Sites $ ___________
- ❏ Refund policy

____

____

____

Make It Personal

Trip dates: | The weather was:

Why I went:

How I got there: (circle all that apply)

I went with:

We stayed in (space, cabin # etc):

Most relaxing day:

Something funny:

Someone we met:

Best story told:

We liked this:

The best food:

Games played:

Something disappointing:

Next time I'll do this differently:

Lockhart State Park

State: Texas　　　City: Lockhart　　　County: Caldwell

Plan your trip: https://tpwd.texas.gov/state-parks/lockhart

Activities:

- ❑ Archery
- ❑ Biking
- ❑ Boating
- ❑ Campfire
- ❑ Caving
- ❑ Disc Golf
- ❑ Fishing
- ❑ Geo Cache
- ❑ Golf
- ❑ Hiking
- ❑ Horseback
- ❑ Hunting
- ❑ Jr. Ranger
- ❑ Park Tours
- ❑ Rock Climbing
- ❑ Stargazing
- ❑ Swimming
- ❑ Wildlife & Birding
- ❑
- ❑

Facilities:

- ❑ ADA
- ❑ Gym
- ❑ Historic Sites
- ❑ Lodge
- ❑ Meeting hall
- ❑ Pavilions
- ❑ Picnic sites
- ❑ Pool
- ❑ Restrooms
- ❑ Showers
- ❑ Visitor center
- ❑ RV Camp
- ❑ Tent Camp
- ❑ Yurt Camp
- ❑ Cabins
- ❑ Lodge rooms
- ❑ Group barracks
- ❑ Screened shelter

Notes:

____

____

____

____

____

____

____

____

____

Get the Facts

- ❑ Phone (512) 398-3479
- ❑ Park Hours

____

- ❑ Reservations? ____Y ____N

date made______________

- ❑ Open year 'round ___Y___N

dates__________________

- ❑ Check in time ___________
- ❑ Check out time __________
- ❑ Dog friendly _____Y _____N
- ❑ Max RV length __________
- ❑ Distance from home

miles: ________________

hours: ________________

- ❑ Address______________

____

____

Fees:

- ❑ Day Use $ ___________
- ❑ Camp Sites $ _________
- ❑ RV Sites $ __________
- ❑ Refund policy

____

____

____

Make It Personal

Trip dates:

The weather was:

Why I went:

How I got there: (circle all that apply)

I went with:

We stayed in (space, cabin # etc):

Most relaxing day:

Something funny:

Someone we met:

Best story told:

We liked this:

The best food:

Games played:

Something disappointing:

Next time I'll do this differently:

Lost Maples State Natural Area

State: Texas **City: Vanderpool** **County: Bandera**

Plan your trip: https://tpwd.texas.gov/state-parks/lost-maples

Activities:

- ❑ Archery
- ❑ Biking
- ❑ Boating
- ❑ Campfire
- ❑ Caving
- ❑ Disc Golf
- ❑ Fishing
- ❑ Geo Cache
- ❑ Golf
- ❑ Hiking
- ❑ Horseback
- ❑ Hunting
- ❑ Jr. Ranger
- ❑ Park Tours
- ❑ Rock Climbing
- ❑ Stargazing
- ❑ Swimming
- ❑ Wildlife & Birding
- ❑
- ❑

Facilities:

- ❑ ADA
- ❑ Gym
- ❑ Historic Sites
- ❑ Lodge
- ❑ Meeting hall
- ❑ Pavilions
- ❑ Picnic sites
- ❑ Pool
- ❑ Restrooms
- ❑ Showers
- ❑ Visitor center
- ❑ RV Camp
- ❑ Tent Camp
- ❑ Yurt Camp
- ❑ Cabins
- ❑ Lodge rooms
- ❑ Group barracks
- ❑ Screened shelter

Notes:

____

____

____

____

____

____

____

____

Get the Facts

- ❑ Phone (830) 966-3413
- ❑ Park Hours

  ____

- ❑ Reservations? _____Y _____N

  date made_______________

- ❑ Open year 'round ___Y___N

  dates__________________

- ❑ Check in time ____________

- ❑ Check out time ___________

- ❑ Dog friendly ______Y ______N

- ❑ Max RV length ___________

- ❑ Distance from home

  miles: _________________

  hours: _________________

- ❑ Address________________

  ____

  ____

Fees:

- ❑ Day Use $ ____________
- ❑ Camp Sites $ __________
- ❑ RV Sites $ ___________
- ❑ Refund policy

  ____

  ____

Make It Personal

Trip dates: The weather was:

Why I went:

How I got there: (circle all that apply)

I went with:

We stayed in (space, cabin # etc):

Most relaxing day:

Something funny:

Someone we met:

Best story told:

We liked this:

The best food:

Games played:

Something disappointing:

Next time I'll do this differently:

Martin Creek Lake State Park

State: Texas   **City: Tatum**   **County: Panola**

Plan your trip: https://tpwd.texas.gov/state-parks/martin-creek-lake

Activities:

- ❑ Archery
- ❑ Biking
- ❑ Boating
- ❑ Campfire
- ❑ Caving
- ❑ Disc Golf
- ❑ Fishing
- ❑ Geo Cache
- ❑ Golf
- ❑ Hiking
- ❑ Horseback
- ❑ Hunting
- ❑ Jr. Ranger
- ❑ Park Tours
- ❑ Rock Climbing
- ❑ Stargazing
- ❑ Swimming
- ❑ Wildlife & Birding
- ❑
- ❑

Facilities:

- ❑ ADA
- ❑ Gym
- ❑ Historic Sites
- ❑ Lodge
- ❑ Meeting hall
- ❑ Pavilions
- ❑ Picnic sites
- ❑ Pool
- ❑ Restrooms
- ❑ Showers
- ❑ Visitor center
- ❑ RV Camp
- ❑ Tent Camp
- ❑ Yurt Camp
- ❑ Cabins
- ❑ Lodge rooms
- ❑ Group barracks
- ❑ Screened shelter

Notes:

____

____

____

____

____

____

____

____

____

Get the Facts

- ❑ Phone (903) 836-4336
- ❑ Park Hours

  ____

- ❑ Reservations? _____Y _____N

  date made________________

- ❑ Open year 'round ___Y___N

  dates____________________

- ❑ Check in time ____________
- ❑ Check out time ___________
- ❑ Dog friendly ______Y ______N
- ❑ Max RV length ___________
- ❑ Distance from home

  miles: __________________

  hours: __________________

- ❑ Address__________________

  ____

  ____

Fees:

- ❑ Day Use $ ____________
- ❑ Camp Sites $ _________
- ❑ RV Sites $ ___________
- ❑ Refund policy

  ____

  ____

  ____

Make It Personal

Trip dates: | The weather was:

Why I went:

How I got there: (circle all that apply)

I went with:

We stayed in (space, cabin # etc):

Most relaxing day:

Something funny:

Someone we met:

Best story told:

We liked this:

The best food:

Games played:

Something disappointing:

Next time I'll do this differently:

Martin Dies, Jr. State Park

State: Texas   **City: Jasper**   **County: Jasper**

Plan your trip: https://tpwd.texas.gov/state-parks/martin-dies-jr

Activities:

- ❑ Archery
- ❑ Biking
- ❑ Boating
- ❑ Campfire
- ❑ Caving
- ❑ Disc Golf
- ❑ Fishing
- ❑ Geo Cache
- ❑ Golf
- ❑ Hiking
- ❑ Horseback
- ❑ Hunting
- ❑ Jr. Ranger
- ❑ Park Tours
- ❑ Rock Climbing
- ❑ Stargazing
- ❑ Swimming
- ❑ Wildlife & Birding
- ❑
- ❑

Facilities:

- ❑ ADA
- ❑ Gym
- ❑ Historic Sites
- ❑ Lodge
- ❑ Meeting hall
- ❑ Pavilions
- ❑ Picnic sites
- ❑ Pool
- ❑ Restrooms
- ❑ Showers
- ❑ Visitor center
- ❑ RV Camp
- ❑ Tent Camp
- ❑ Yurt Camp
- ❑ Cabins
- ❑ Lodge rooms
- ❑ Group barracks
- ❑ Screened shelter

Notes:

____

____

____

____

____

____

____

____

Get the Facts

- ❑ Phone (409) 384-5231
- ❑ Park Hours

  ____

- ❑ Reservations? _____Y _____N

  date made_______________

- ❑ Open year 'round ___Y___N

  dates__________________

- ❑ Check in time ___________

- ❑ Check out time __________

- ❑ Dog friendly _____Y _____N

- ❑ Max RV length __________

- ❑ Distance from home

  miles: ________________

  hours: ________________

- ❑ Address________________

  ____

  ____

Fees:

- ❑ Day Use $ ___________
- ❑ Camp Sites $ _________
- ❑ RV Sites $ ___________
- ❑ Refund policy

  ____

  ____

Make It Personal

Trip dates: The weather was:

Why I went:

How I got there: (circle all that apply)

I went with:

We stayed in (space, cabin # etc):

Most relaxing day:

Something funny:

Someone we met:

Best story told:

We liked this:

The best food:

Games played:

Something disappointing:

Next time I'll do this differently:

McKinney Falls State Park

State: Texas   City: Austin   County: Travis

Plan your trip: https://tpwd.texas.gov/state-parks/mckinney-falls

Activities:

- ❑ Archery
- ❑ Biking
- ❑ Boating
- ❑ Campfire
- ❑ Caving
- ❑ Disc Golf
- ❑ Fishing
- ❑ Geo Cache
- ❑ Golf
- ❑ Hiking
- ❑ Horseback
- ❑ Hunting
- ❑ Jr. Ranger
- ❑ Park Tours
- ❑ Rock Climbing
- ❑ Stargazing
- ❑ Swimming
- ❑ Wildlife & Birding
- ❑
- ❑

Facilities:

- ❑ ADA
- ❑ Gym
- ❑ Historic Sites
- ❑ Lodge
- ❑ Meeting hall
- ❑ Pavilions
- ❑ Picnic sites
- ❑ Pool
- ❑ Restrooms
- ❑ Showers
- ❑ Visitor center
- ❑ RV Camp
- ❑ Tent Camp
- ❑ Yurt Camp
- ❑ Cabins
- ❑ Lodge rooms
- ❑ Group barracks
- ❑ Screened shelter

Notes:

____

____

____

____

____

____

____

____

Get the Facts

- ❑ Phone (512) 243-1643
- ❑ Park Hours

____

- ❑ Reservations? _____Y _____N

date made________________

- ❑ Open year 'round ___Y___N

dates____________________

- ❑ Check in time ____________
- ❑ Check out time ___________
- ❑ Dog friendly ______Y _____N
- ❑ Max RV length ___________
- ❑ Distance from home

miles: ___________________

hours: ___________________

- ❑ Address________________

____

____

Fees:

- ❑ Day Use $ ___________
- ❑ Camp Sites $ __________
- ❑ RV Sites $ ___________
- ❑ Refund policy

____

____

____

Make It Personal

Trip dates: | The weather was: 

Why I went:

How I got there: (circle all that apply)

I went with:

We stayed in (space, cabin # etc):

Most relaxing day:

Something funny:

Someone we met:

Best story told:

We liked this:

The best food:

Games played:

Something disappointing:

Next time I'll do this differently:

Meridian State Park

State: Texas   **City: Meridian**   **County: Bosque**

Plan your trip: https://tpwd.texas.gov/state-parks/meridian

Activities:

- ❑ Archery
- ❑ Biking
- ❑ Boating
- ❑ Campfire
- ❑ Caving
- ❑ Disc Golf
- ❑ Fishing
- ❑ Geo Cache
- ❑ Golf
- ❑ Hiking
- ❑ Horseback
- ❑ Hunting
- ❑ Jr. Ranger
- ❑ Park Tours
- ❑ Rock Climbing
- ❑ Stargazing
- ❑ Swimming
- ❑ Wildlife & Birding
- ❑
- ❑

Facilities:

- ❑ ADA
- ❑ Gym
- ❑ Historic Sites
- ❑ Lodge
- ❑ Meeting hall
- ❑ Pavilions
- ❑ Picnic sites
- ❑ Pool
- ❑ Restrooms
- ❑ Showers
- ❑ Visitor center
- ❑ RV Camp
- ❑ Tent Camp
- ❑ Yurt Camp
- ❑ Cabins
- ❑ Lodge rooms
- ❑ Group barracks
- ❑ Screened shelter

Notes:

____

____

____

____

____

____

____

____

Get the Facts

- ❑ Phone (254) 435-2536
- ❑ Park Hours

  ____

- ❑ Reservations? _____Y _____N

  date made_______________

- ❑ Open year 'round ___Y___N

  dates____________________

- ❑ Check in time ____________

- ❑ Check out time ___________

- ❑ Dog friendly ______Y ______N

- ❑ Max RV length ___________

- ❑ Distance from home

  miles: __________________

  hours: __________________

- ❑ Address_________________

  ____

  ____

Fees:

- ❑ Day Use $ ____________
- ❑ Camp Sites $ __________
- ❑ RV Sites $ ___________
- ❑ Refund policy

  ____

  ____

Make It Personal

Trip dates: | The weather was:

Why I went:

How I got there: (circle all that apply)

I went with:

We stayed in (space, cabin # etc):

Most relaxing day:

Something funny:

Someone we met:

Best story told:

We liked this:

The best food:

Games played:

Something disappointing:

Next time I'll do this differently:

Mission Tejas State Park

State: Texas   **City: Grapeland**   **County: Houston**

Plan your trip: https://tpwd.texas.gov/state-parks/mission-tejas

Activities:

- ❑ Archery
- ❑ Biking
- ❑ Boating
- ❑ Campfire
- ❑ Caving
- ❑ Disc Golf
- ❑ Fishing
- ❑ Geo Cache
- ❑ Golf
- ❑ Hiking
- ❑ Horseback
- ❑ Hunting
- ❑ Jr. Ranger
- ❑ Park Tours
- ❑ Rock Climbing
- ❑ Stargazing
- ❑ Swimming
- ❑ Wildlife & Birding
- ❑
- ❑

Facilities:

- ❑ ADA
- ❑ Gym
- ❑ Historic Sites
- ❑ Lodge
- ❑ Meeting hall
- ❑ Pavilions
- ❑ Picnic sites
- ❑ Pool
- ❑ Restrooms
- ❑ Showers
- ❑ Visitor center
- ❑ RV Camp
- ❑ Tent Camp
- ❑ Yurt Camp
- ❑ Cabins
- ❑ Lodge rooms
- ❑ Group barracks
- ❑ Screened shelter

Notes:

____

____

____

____

____

____

____

____

____

Get the Facts

- ❑ Phone (936) 687-2394
- ❑ Park Hours

____

- ❑ Reservations? _____Y _____N

  date made_______________

- ❑ Open year 'round ___Y___N

  dates___________________

- ❑ Check in time ____________
- ❑ Check out time ___________
- ❑ Dog friendly _____Y _____N
- ❑ Max RV length __________
- ❑ Distance from home

  miles: ________________

  hours: ________________

- ❑ Address________________

____

____

Fees:

- ❑ Day Use $ ___________
- ❑ Camp Sites $ _________
- ❑ RV Sites $ ___________
- ❑ Refund policy

____

____

____

Make It Personal

Trip dates: ___________________ | The weather was:

Why I went: ___________________

How I got there: (circle all that apply)

I went with: ___________________

We stayed in (space, cabin # etc): ___________________

Most relaxing day: ___________________

Something funny: ___________________

Someone we met: ___________________

Best story told: ___________________

We liked this: ___________________

The best food: ___________________

Games played: ___________________

Something disappointing: ___________________

Next time I'll do this differently: ___________________

Monahans Sandhills State Park

State: Texas   **City: Monahans**   **County: Ward**

Plan your trip: https://tpwd.texas.gov/state-parks/monahans-sandhills

Activities:

- ❏ Archery
- ❏ Biking
- ❏ Boating
- ❏ Campfire
- ❏ Caving
- ❏ Disc Golf
- ❏ Fishing
- ❏ Geo Cache
- ❏ Golf
- ❏ Hiking
- ❏ Horseback
- ❏ Hunting
- ❏ Jr. Ranger
- ❏ Park Tours
- ❏ Rock Climbing
- ❏ Stargazing
- ❏ Swimming
- ❏ Wildlife & Birding
- ❏
- ❏

Facilities:

- ❏ ADA
- ❏ Gym
- ❏ Historic Sites
- ❏ Lodge
- ❏ Meeting hall
- ❏ Pavilions
- ❏ Picnic sites
- ❏ Pool
- ❏ Restrooms
- ❏ Showers
- ❏ Visitor center
- ❏ RV Camp
- ❏ Tent Camp
- ❏ Yurt Camp
- ❏ Cabins
- ❏ Lodge rooms
- ❏ Group barracks
- ❏ Screened shelter

Notes:

____

____

____

____

____

____

____

____

Get the Facts

- ❏ Phone (432) 943-2092
- ❏ Park Hours

____

- ❏ Reservations? _____Y _____N

  date made_______________

- ❏ Open year 'round ___Y___N

  dates___________________

- ❏ Check in time ____________
- ❏ Check out time ___________
- ❏ Dog friendly ______Y ______N
- ❏ Max RV length ___________
- ❏ Distance from home

  miles: ________________

  hours: ________________

- ❏ Address________________

____

____

Fees:

- ❏ Day Use $ ___________
- ❏ Camp Sites $ _________
- ❏ RV Sites $ ___________
- ❏ Refund policy

____

____

Make It Personal

Trip dates: ___________________ | The weather was: ☀ ⛅ 🌦 🌧 ⛈ 🌫 💨 🌡

Why I went: ____

____

How I got there: (circle all that apply)

I went with: ____

We stayed in (space, cabin # etc): __________________________

Most relaxing day: ____

____

Something funny: ____

____

Someone we met: ____

____

Best story told: ____

____

We liked this: ____

____

The best food: ____

____

Games played: ____

____

Something disappointing: ___________________________________

____

Next time I'll do this differently: ___________________________

____

Mother Neff State Park

State: Texas   City: Moody   County: McLennan

Plan your trip: https://tpwd.texas.gov/state-parks/mother-neff

Activities:

- ❑ Archery
- ❑ Biking
- ❑ Boating
- ❑ Campfire
- ❑ Caving
- ❑ Disc Golf
- ❑ Fishing
- ❑ Geo Cache
- ❑ Golf
- ❑ Hiking
- ❑ Horseback
- ❑ Hunting
- ❑ Jr. Ranger
- ❑ Park Tours
- ❑ Rock Climbing
- ❑ Stargazing
- ❑ Swimming
- ❑ Wildlife & Birding
- ❑
- ❑

Facilities:

- ❑ ADA
- ❑ Gym
- ❑ Historic Sites
- ❑ Lodge
- ❑ Meeting hall
- ❑ Pavilions
- ❑ Picnic sites
- ❑ Pool
- ❑ Restrooms
- ❑ Showers
- ❑ Visitor center
- ❑ RV Camp
- ❑ Tent Camp
- ❑ Yurt Camp
- ❑ Cabins
- ❑ Lodge rooms
- ❑ Group barracks
- ❑ Screened shelter

Notes:

____

____

____

____

____

____

____

____

Get the Facts

- ❑ Phone (254) 853-2389
- ❑ Park Hours

____

- ❑ Reservations? _____Y _____N

date made______________

- ❑ Open year 'round ___Y___N

dates__________________

- ❑ Check in time ____________
- ❑ Check out time __________
- ❑ Dog friendly _____Y _____N
- ❑ Max RV length __________
- ❑ Distance from home

miles: __________________

hours: __________________

- ❑ Address________________

____

Fees:

- ❑ Day Use $ ___________
- ❑ Camp Sites $ _________
- ❑ RV Sites $ ___________
- ❑ Refund policy

____

____

____

Make It Personal

Trip dates:

The weather was:

Why I went:

How I got there: (circle all that apply)

I went with:

We stayed in (space, cabin # etc):

Most relaxing day:

Something funny:

Someone we met:

Best story told:

We liked this:

The best food:

Games played:

Something disappointing:

Next time I'll do this differently:

Mustang Island State Park

State: Texas   City: Corpus Christi   County: Nueces

Plan your trip: https://tpwd.texas.gov/state-parks/mustang-island

Activities:

- ❑ Archery
- ❑ Biking
- ❑ Boating
- ❑ Campfire
- ❑ Caving
- ❑ Disc Golf
- ❑ Fishing
- ❑ Geo Cache
- ❑ Golf
- ❑ Hiking
- ❑ Horseback
- ❑ Hunting
- ❑ Jr. Ranger
- ❑ Park Tours
- ❑ Rock Climbing
- ❑ Stargazing
- ❑ Swimming
- ❑ Wildlife & Birding
- ❑
- ❑

Facilities:

- ❑ ADA
- ❑ Gym
- ❑ Historic Sites
- ❑ Lodge
- ❑ Meeting hall
- ❑ Pavilions
- ❑ Picnic sites
- ❑ Pool
- ❑ Restrooms
- ❑ Showers
- ❑ Visitor center
- ❑ RV Camp
- ❑ Tent Camp
- ❑ Yurt Camp
- ❑ Cabins
- ❑ Lodge rooms
- ❑ Group barracks
- ❑ Screened shelter

Notes:

____

____

____

____

____

____

____

____

Get the Facts

- ❑ Phone (361) 749-5246
- ❑ Park Hours

  ____

- ❑ Reservations? ____Y ____N

  date made____________

- ❑ Open year 'round ___Y___N

  dates__________________

- ❑ Check in time ___________

- ❑ Check out time __________

- ❑ Dog friendly _____Y _____N

- ❑ Max RV length __________

- ❑ Distance from home

  miles: ________________

  hours: ________________

- ❑ Address_______________

  ____

  ____

Fees:

- ❑ Day Use $ __________
- ❑ Camp Sites $ _________
- ❑ RV Sites $ __________
- ❑ Refund policy

  ____

  ____

Make It Personal

Trip dates: | The weather was: 

Why I went:

How I got there: (circle all that apply)

I went with:

We stayed in (space, cabin # etc):

Most relaxing day:

Something funny:

Someone we met:

Best story told:

We liked this:

The best food:

Games played:

Something disappointing:

Next time I'll do this differently:

Palmetto State Park

State: Texas   City: Gonzales   County: Gonzales

Plan your trip: https://tpwd.texas.gov/state-parks/palmetto

Activities:

- ❑ Archery
- ❑ Biking
- ❑ Boating
- ❑ Campfire
- ❑ Caving
- ❑ Disc Golf
- ❑ Fishing
- ❑ Geo Cache
- ❑ Golf
- ❑ Hiking
- ❑ Horseback
- ❑ Hunting
- ❑ Jr. Ranger
- ❑ Park Tours
- ❑ Rock Climbing
- ❑ Stargazing
- ❑ Swimming
- ❑ Wildlife & Birding
- ❑
- ❑

Facilities:

- ❑ ADA
- ❑ Gym
- ❑ Historic Sites
- ❑ Lodge
- ❑ Meeting hall
- ❑ Pavilions
- ❑ Picnic sites
- ❑ Pool
- ❑ Restrooms
- ❑ Showers
- ❑ Visitor center
- ❑ RV Camp
- ❑ Tent Camp
- ❑ Yurt Camp
- ❑ Cabins
- ❑ Lodge rooms
- ❑ Group barracks
- ❑ Screened shelter

Get the Facts

- ❑ Phone (830) 672-3266
- ❑ Park Hours

  ____

- ❑ Reservations? ____Y ____N

  date made_______________

- ❑ Open year 'round ___Y___N

  dates___________________

- ❑ Check in time ___________
- ❑ Check out time __________
- ❑ Dog friendly ______Y _____N
- ❑ Max RV length __________
- ❑ Distance from home

  miles: _________________

  hours: _________________

- ❑ Address________________

  ____

  ____

Fees:

- ❑ Day Use $ ___________
- ❑ Camp Sites $ _________
- ❑ RV Sites $ ___________
- ❑ Refund policy

  ____

  ____

Notes:

____

____

____

____

____

____

____

____

Make It Personal

Trip dates: | The weather was:

Why I went:

How I got there: (circle all that apply)

I went with:

We stayed in (space, cabin # etc):

Most relaxing day:

Something funny:

Someone we met:

Best story told:

We liked this:

The best food:

Games played:

Something disappointing:

Next time I'll do this differently:

Palo Duro Canyon State Park

State: Texas   **City: Canyon**   **County: Randall**

Plan your trip: https://tpwd.texas.gov/state-parks/palo-duro-canyon

Activities:

- ❑ Archery
- ❑ Biking
- ❑ Boating
- ❑ Campfire
- ❑ Caving
- ❑ Disc Golf
- ❑ Fishing
- ❑ Geo Cache
- ❑ Golf
- ❑ Hiking
- ❑ Horseback
- ❑ Hunting
- ❑ Jr. Ranger
- ❑ Park Tours
- ❑ Rock Climbing
- ❑ Stargazing
- ❑ Swimming
- ❑ Wildlife & Birding
- ❑
- ❑

Facilities:

- ❑ ADA
- ❑ Gym
- ❑ Historic Sites
- ❑ Lodge
- ❑ Meeting hall
- ❑ Pavilions
- ❑ Picnic sites
- ❑ Pool
- ❑ Restrooms
- ❑ Showers
- ❑ Visitor center
- ❑ RV Camp
- ❑ Tent Camp
- ❑ Yurt Camp
- ❑ Cabins
- ❑ Lodge rooms
- ❑ Group barracks
- ❑ Screened shelter

Notes:

____

____

____

____

____

____

____

____

____

Get the Facts

- ❑ Phone (806) 488-2227
- ❑ Park Hours

  ____

- ❑ Reservations? _____Y _____N

  date made_______________

- ❑ Open year 'round ___Y___N

  dates_________________

- ❑ Check in time ___________
- ❑ Check out time __________
- ❑ Dog friendly _____Y _____N
- ❑ Max RV length _________
- ❑ Distance from home

  miles: ________________

  hours: ________________

- ❑ Address_______________

  ____

  ____

Fees:

- ❑ Day Use $ __________
- ❑ Camp Sites $ _________
- ❑ RV Sites $ __________
- ❑ Refund policy

  ____

  ____

  ____

Make It Personal

Trip dates: ___________________ | The weather was:

Why I went: ___________________

____

How I got there: (circle all that apply)

____

I went with: ___________________

We stayed in (space, cabin # etc): ___________________

Most relaxing day: ___________________

____

Something funny: ___________________

____

Someone we met: ___________________

____

Best story told: ___________________

____

We liked this: ___________________

____

The best food: ___________________

____

Games played: ___________________

____

Something disappointing: ___________________

____

Next time I'll do this differently: ___________________

____

Pedernales Falls State Park

State: Texas   City: Johnson City   County: Blanco

Plan your trip: https://tpwd.texas.gov/state-parks/pedernales-falls

Activities:

- ❑ Archery
- ❑ Biking
- ❑ Boating
- ❑ Campfire
- ❑ Caving
- ❑ Disc Golf
- ❑ Fishing
- ❑ Geo Cache
- ❑ Golf
- ❑ Hiking
- ❑ Horseback
- ❑ Hunting
- ❑ Jr. Ranger
- ❑ Park Tours
- ❑ Rock Climbing
- ❑ Stargazing
- ❑ Swimming
- ❑ Wildlife & Birding
- ❑
- ❑

Facilities:

- ❑ ADA
- ❑ Gym
- ❑ Historic Sites
- ❑ Lodge
- ❑ Meeting hall
- ❑ Pavilions
- ❑ Picnic sites
- ❑ Pool
- ❑ Restrooms
- ❑ Showers
- ❑ Visitor center
- ❑ RV Camp
- ❑ Tent Camp
- ❑ Yurt Camp
- ❑ Cabins
- ❑ Lodge rooms
- ❑ Group barracks
- ❑ Screened shelter

Notes:

____

____

____

____

____

____

____

____

Get the Facts

- ❑ Phone (830) 868-7304
- ❑ Park Hours

____

- ❑ Reservations? _____Y _____N

date made_______________

- ❑ Open year 'round ___Y___N

dates___________________

- ❑ Check in time ____________
- ❑ Check out time ___________
- ❑ Dog friendly _____Y _____N
- ❑ Max RV length ___________
- ❑ Distance from home

miles: ___________________

hours: ___________________

- ❑ Address________________

____

____

Fees:

- ❑ Day Use $ ____________
- ❑ Camp Sites $ __________
- ❑ RV Sites $ ____________
- ❑ Refund policy

____

____

____

Make It Personal

Trip dates: | The weather was: ☀ ⛅ 🌦 🌧 ⛈ 🌫 🌬 🌡🌡

Why I went:

How I got there: (circle all that apply)

I went with:

We stayed in (space, cabin # etc):

Most relaxing day:

Something funny:

Someone we met:

Best story told:

We liked this:

The best food:

Games played:

Something disappointing:

Next time I'll do this differently:

Possum Kingdom State Park
State: Texas   City: Caddo   County: Stephens

Plan your trip: https://tpwd.texas.gov/state-parks/possum-kingdom

Activities:

- ❑ Archery
- ❑ Biking
- ❑ Boating
- ❑ Campfire
- ❑ Caving
- ❑ Disc Golf
- ❑ Fishing
- ❑ Geo Cache
- ❑ Golf
- ❑ Hiking
- ❑ Horseback
- ❑ Hunting
- ❑ Jr. Ranger
- ❑ Park Tours
- ❑ Rock Climbing
- ❑ Stargazing
- ❑ Swimming
- ❑ Wildlife & Birding
- ❑
- ❑

Facilities:

- ❑ ADA
- ❑ Gym
- ❑ Historic Sites
- ❑ Lodge
- ❑ Meeting hall
- ❑ Pavilions
- ❑ Picnic sites
- ❑ Pool
- ❑ Restrooms
- ❑ Showers
- ❑ Visitor center
- ❑ RV Camp
- ❑ Tent Camp
- ❑ Yurt Camp
- ❑ Cabins
- ❑ Lodge rooms
- ❑ Group barracks
- ❑ Screened shelter

Notes:

____
____
____
____
____
____
____
____
____
____
____
____
____

Get the Facts

- ❑ Phone (830) 868-7304
- ❑ Park Hours

  ____

- ❑ Reservations? _____Y _____N

  date made________________

- ❑ Open year 'round ___Y___N

  dates____________________

- ❑ Check in time ____________
- ❑ Check out time __________
- ❑ Dog friendly _____Y _____N
- ❑ Max RV length __________
- ❑ Distance from home

  miles: __________________

  hours: __________________

- ❑ Address________________

  ____

  ____

Fees:

- ❑ Day Use $ ___________
- ❑ Camp Sites $ _________
- ❑ RV Sites $ ___________
- ❑ Refund policy

  ____

  ____

  ____

Make It Personal

Trip dates: ___________________ | The weather was:

____

Why I went:

____

____

How I got there: (circle all that apply)

____

I went with:

____

We stayed in (space, cabin # etc):

____

Most relaxing day:

____

Something funny:

____

Someone we met:

____

Best story told:

____

We liked this:

____

The best food:

____

Games played:

____

Something disappointing:

____

Next time I'll do this differently:

____

Purtis Creek State Park

State: Texas   **City: Eustace**   **County: Henderson**

Plan your trip: https://tpwd.texas.gov/state-parks/purtis-creek

Activities:

- ❏ Archery
- ❏ Biking
- ❏ Boating
- ❏ Campfire
- ❏ Caving
- ❏ Disc Golf
- ❏ Fishing
- ❏ Geo Cache
- ❏ Golf
- ❏ Hiking
- ❏ Horseback
- ❏ Hunting
- ❏ Jr. Ranger
- ❏ Park Tours
- ❏ Rock Climbing
- ❏ Stargazing
- ❏ Swimming
- ❏ Wildlife & Birding
- ❏
- ❏

Facilities:

- ❏ ADA
- ❏ Gym
- ❏ Historic Sites
- ❏ Lodge
- ❏ Meeting hall
- ❏ Pavilions
- ❏ Picnic sites
- ❏ Pool
- ❏ Restrooms
- ❏ Showers
- ❏ Visitor center
- ❏ RV Camp
- ❏ Tent Camp
- ❏ Yurt Camp
- ❏ Cabins
- ❏ Lodge rooms
- ❏ Group barracks
- ❏ Screened shelter

Notes:

____

____

____

____

____

____

____

____

____

Get the Facts

- ❏ Phone (903) 425-2332
- ❏ Park Hours

  ____

- ❏ Reservations? _____Y _____N

  date made_______________
- ❏ Open year 'round ___Y___N

  dates_________________
- ❏ Check in time ___________
- ❏ Check out time __________
- ❏ Dog friendly _____Y _____N
- ❏ Max RV length __________
- ❏ Distance from home

  miles: ________________

  hours: ________________
- ❏ Address_______________

  ____

  ____

Fees:

- ❏ Day Use $ __________
- ❏ Camp Sites $ ________
- ❏ RV Sites $ __________
- ❏ Refund policy

  ____

  ____

  ____

Make It Personal

Trip dates: _______________ | The weather was:

Why I went: _______________

How I got there: (circle all that apply)

I went with: _______________

We stayed in (space, cabin # etc): _______________

Most relaxing day: _______________

Something funny: _______________

Someone we met: _______________

Best story told: _______________

We liked this: _______________

The best food: _______________

Games played: _______________

Something disappointing: _______________

Next time I'll do this differently: _______________

Ray Roberts Lake State Park-Isle du Bois
State: Texas   City: Pilot Point   County: Denton

Plan your trip: https://tpwd.texas.gov/state-parks/ray-roberts-lake

Activities:

- ❏ Archery
- ❏ Biking
- ❏ Boating
- ❏ Campfire
- ❏ Caving
- ❏ Disc Golf
- ❏ Fishing
- ❏ Geo Cache
- ❏ Golf
- ❏ Hiking
- ❏ Horseback
- ❏ Hunting
- ❏ Jr. Ranger
- ❏ Park Tours
- ❏ Rock Climbing
- ❏ Stargazing
- ❏ Swimming
- ❏ Wildlife & Birding
- ❏
- ❏

Facilities:

- ❏ ADA
- ❏ Gym
- ❏ Historic Sites
- ❏ Lodge
- ❏ Meeting hall
- ❏ Pavilions
- ❏ Picnic sites
- ❏ Pool
- ❏ Restrooms
- ❏ Showers
- ❏ Visitor center
- ❏ RV Camp
- ❏ Tent Camp
- ❏ Yurt Camp
- ❏ Cabins
- ❏ Lodge rooms
- ❏ Group barracks
- ❏ Screened shelter

Notes:

____

____

____

____

____

____

____

____

Get the Facts

- ❏ Phone (940) 686-2148
- ❏ Park Hours

  ____

- ❏ Reservations? _____Y _____N

  date made________________

- ❏ Open year 'round ___Y___N

  dates____________________

- ❏ Check in time ____________

- ❏ Check out time __________

- ❏ Dog friendly ______Y _____N

- ❏ Max RV length __________

- ❏ Distance from home

  miles: __________________

  hours: __________________

- ❏ Address________________

  ____

Fees:

- ❏ Day Use $ ____________
- ❏ Camp Sites $ _________
- ❏ RV Sites $ ___________
- ❏ Refund policy

  ____

  ____

  ____

Make It Personal

Trip dates: | The weather was:

Why I went:

How I got there: (circle all that apply)

I went with:

We stayed in (space, cabin # etc):

Most relaxing day:

Something funny:

Someone we met:

Best story told:

We liked this:

The best food:

Games played:

Something disappointing:

Next time I'll do this differently:

Ray Roberts Lake State Park - Johnson

State: Texas   City: Valley View   County: Cooke

Plan your trip: https://tpwd.texas.gov/state-parks/ray-roberts-lake

Activities:

- ❑ Archery
- ❑ Biking
- ❑ Boating
- ❑ Campfire
- ❑ Caving
- ❑ Disc Golf
- ❑ Fishing
- ❑ Geo Cache
- ❑ Golf
- ❑ Hiking
- ❑ Horseback
- ❑ Hunting
- ❑ Jr. Ranger
- ❑ Park Tours
- ❑ Rock Climbing
- ❑ Stargazing
- ❑ Swimming
- ❑ Wildlife & Birding
- ❑
- ❑

Facilities:

- ❑ ADA
- ❑ Gym
- ❑ Historic Sites
- ❑ Lodge
- ❑ Meeting hall
- ❑ Pavilions
- ❑ Picnic sites
- ❑ Pool
- ❑ Restrooms
- ❑ Showers
- ❑ Visitor center
- ❑ RV Camp
- ❑ Tent Camp
- ❑ Yurt Camp
- ❑ Cabins
- ❑ Lodge rooms
- ❑ Group barracks
- ❑ Screened shelter

Get the Facts

- ❑ Phone (940) 637-2294
- ❑ Park Hours

  ____

- ❑ Reservations? ____Y ____N

  date made_______________

- ❑ Open year 'round ___Y___N

  dates__________________

- ❑ Check in time ___________
- ❑ Check out time __________
- ❑ Dog friendly _____Y _____N
- ❑ Max RV length __________
- ❑ Distance from home

  miles: ________________

  hours: ________________

- ❑ Address_______________

  ____

Fees:

- ❑ Day Use $ __________
- ❑ Camp Sites $ _________
- ❑ RV Sites $ __________
- ❑ Refund policy

  ____

  ____

  ____

Notes:

____

____

____

____

____

____

____

____

Make It Personal

Trip dates: | The weather was:

Why I went:

How I got there: (circle all that apply)

I went with:

We stayed in (space, cabin # etc):

Most relaxing day:

Something funny:

Someone we met:

Best story told:

We liked this:

The best food:

Games played:

Something disappointing:

Next time I'll do this differently:

San Angelo State Park

State: Texas   **City: San Angelo**   **County: Tom Green**

Plan your trip: https://tpwd.texas.gov/state-parks/san-angelo

Activities:

- ❑ Archery
- ❑ Biking
- ❑ Boating
- ❑ Campfire
- ❑ Caving
- ❑ Disc Golf
- ❑ Fishing
- ❑ Geo Cache
- ❑ Golf
- ❑ Hiking
- ❑ Horseback
- ❑ Hunting
- ❑ Jr. Ranger
- ❑ Park Tours
- ❑ Rock Climbing
- ❑ Stargazing
- ❑ Swimming
- ❑ Wildlife & Birding
- ❑
- ❑

Facilities:

- ❑ ADA
- ❑ Gym
- ❑ Historic Sites
- ❑ Lodge
- ❑ Meeting hall
- ❑ Pavilions
- ❑ Picnic sites
- ❑ Pool
- ❑ Restrooms
- ❑ Showers
- ❑ Visitor center
- ❑ RV Camp
- ❑ Tent Camp
- ❑ Yurt Camp
- ❑ Cabins
- ❑ Lodge rooms
- ❑ Group barracks
- ❑ Screened shelter

Get the Facts

- ❑ Phone (325) 949-4757
- ❑ Park Hours

  ____

- ❑ Reservations? _____Y _____N

  date made_______________
- ❑ Open year 'round ___Y___N

  dates__________________
- ❑ Check in time ___________
- ❑ Check out time __________
- ❑ Dog friendly _____Y _____N
- ❑ Max RV length __________
- ❑ Distance from home

  miles: ________________

  hours: ________________
- ❑ Address_______________

  ____

  ____

Fees:

- ❑ Day Use $ ___________
- ❑ Camp Sites $ _________
- ❑ RV Sites $ ___________
- ❑ Refund policy

  ____

  ____

Notes:

____

____

____

____

____

____

____

____

____

Make It Personal

Trip dates: | The weather was: 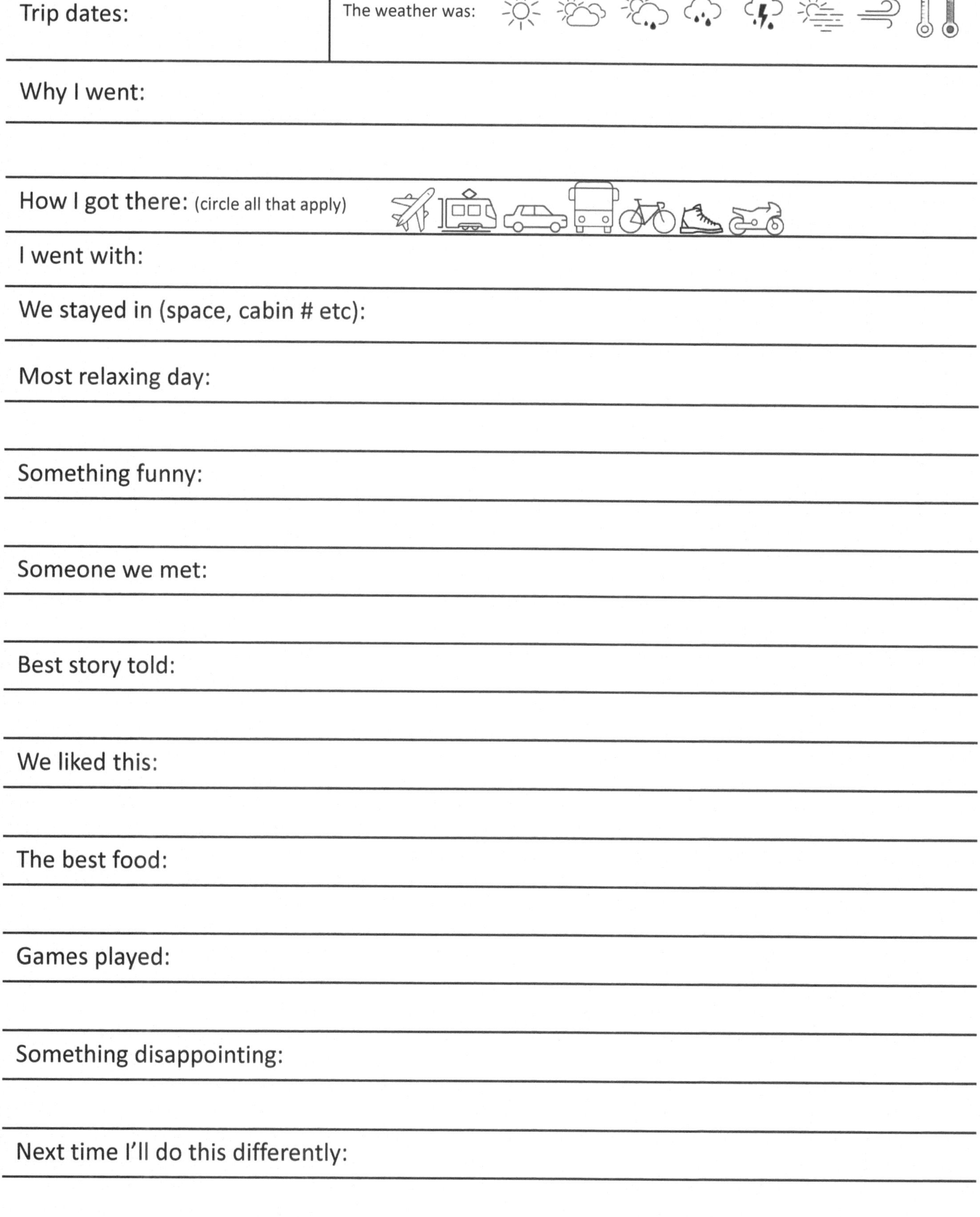

Why I went:

How I got there: (circle all that apply)

I went with:

We stayed in (space, cabin # etc):

Most relaxing day:

Something funny:

Someone we met:

Best story told:

We liked this:

The best food:

Games played:

Something disappointing:

Next time I'll do this differently:

Sea Rim State Park
State: Texas   City: Sabine Pass   County: Jefferson

Plan your trip: https://tpwd.texas.gov/state-parks/sea-rim

Activities:

- ❑ Archery
- ❑ Biking
- ❑ Boating
- ❑ Campfire
- ❑ Caving
- ❑ Disc Golf
- ❑ Fishing
- ❑ Geo Cache
- ❑ Golf
- ❑ Hiking
- ❑ Horseback
- ❑ Hunting
- ❑ Jr. Ranger
- ❑ Park Tours
- ❑ Rock Climbing
- ❑ Stargazing
- ❑ Swimming
- ❑ Wildlife & Birding
- ❑
- ❑

Facilities:

- ❑ ADA
- ❑ Gym
- ❑ Historic Sites
- ❑ Lodge
- ❑ Meeting hall
- ❑ Pavilions
- ❑ Picnic sites
- ❑ Pool
- ❑ Restrooms
- ❑ Showers
- ❑ Visitor center
- ❑ RV Camp
- ❑ Tent Camp
- ❑ Yurt Camp
- ❑ Cabins
- ❑ Lodge rooms
- ❑ Group barracks
- ❑ Screened shelter

Notes:

____

____

____

____

____

____

____

____

Get the Facts

- ❑ Phone (409) 971-2559
- ❑ Park Hours

____

- ❑ Reservations? _____Y _____N

date made______________

- ❑ Open year 'round ___Y___N

dates__________________

- ❑ Check in time ___________
- ❑ Check out time __________
- ❑ Dog friendly ______Y ______N
- ❑ Max RV length __________
- ❑ Distance from home

miles: ________________

hours: ________________

- ❑ Address________________

____

____

Fees:

- ❑ Day Use $ ___________
- ❑ Camp Sites $ _________
- ❑ RV Sites $ ___________
- ❑ Refund policy

____

____

Make It Personal

Trip dates: | The weather was:

Why I went:

How I got there: (circle all that apply)

I went with:

We stayed in (space, cabin # etc):

Most relaxing day:

Something funny:

Someone we met:

Best story told:

We liked this:

The best food:

Games played:

Something disappointing:

Next time I'll do this differently:

Seminole Canyon State Park & Historic Site

State: Texas   City: Comstock   County: Val Verde

Plan your trip: https://tpwd.texas.gov/state-parks/seminole-canyon

Activities:

- ❑ Archery
- ❑ Biking
- ❑ Boating
- ❑ Campfire
- ❑ Caving
- ❑ Disc Golf
- ❑ Fishing
- ❑ Geo Cache
- ❑ Golf
- ❑ Hiking
- ❑ Horseback
- ❑ Hunting
- ❑ Jr. Ranger
- ❑ Park Tours
- ❑ Rock Climbing
- ❑ Stargazing
- ❑ Swimming
- ❑ Wildlife & Birding
- ❑
- ❑

Facilities:

- ❑ ADA
- ❑ Gym
- ❑ Historic Sites
- ❑ Lodge
- ❑ Meeting hall
- ❑ Pavilions
- ❑ Picnic sites
- ❑ Pool
- ❑ Restrooms
- ❑ Showers
- ❑ Visitor center
- ❑ RV Camp
- ❑ Tent Camp
- ❑ Yurt Camp
- ❑ Cabins
- ❑ Lodge rooms
- ❑ Group barracks
- ❑ Screened shelter

Notes:

____

____

____

____

____

____

____

____

____

Get the Facts

- ❑ Phone (432) 292-4464
- ❑ Park Hours

____

- ❑ Reservations? _____Y _____N

date made_______________

- ❑ Open year 'round ___Y___N

dates___________________

- ❑ Check in time ____________
- ❑ Check out time ___________
- ❑ Dog friendly _____Y _____N
- ❑ Max RV length ___________
- ❑ Distance from home

miles: __________________

hours: __________________

- ❑ Address________________

____

____

Fees:

- ❑ Day Use $ ___________
- ❑ Camp Sites $ _________
- ❑ RV Sites $ ___________
- ❑ Refund policy

____

____

Make It Personal

Trip dates: | The weather was:

Why I went:

How I got there: (circle all that apply)

I went with:

We stayed in (space, cabin # etc):

Most relaxing day:

Something funny:

Someone we met:

Best story told:

We liked this:

The best food:

Games played:

Something disappointing:

Next time I'll do this differently:

South Llano River State Park

State: Texas   City: Junction   County: Kimble

Plan your trip: https://tpwd.texas.gov/state-parks/south-llano-river

Activities:

- ❑ Archery
- ❑ Biking
- ❑ Boating
- ❑ Campfire
- ❑ Caving
- ❑ Disc Golf
- ❑ Fishing
- ❑ Geo Cache
- ❑ Golf
- ❑ Hiking
- ❑ Horseback
- ❑ Hunting
- ❑ Jr. Ranger
- ❑ Park Tours
- ❑ Rock Climbing
- ❑ Stargazing
- ❑ Swimming
- ❑ Wildlife & Birding
- ❑
- ❑

Facilities:

- ❑ ADA
- ❑ Gym
- ❑ Historic Sites
- ❑ Lodge
- ❑ Meeting hall
- ❑ Pavilions
- ❑ Picnic sites
- ❑ Pool
- ❑ Restrooms
- ❑ Showers
- ❑ Visitor center
- ❑ RV Camp
- ❑ Tent Camp
- ❑ Yurt Camp
- ❑ Cabins
- ❑ Lodge rooms
- ❑ Group barracks
- ❑ Screened shelter

Get the Facts

- ❑ Phone (325) 446-3994
- ❑ Park Hours

  ____

- ❑ Reservations? _____Y _____N

  date made_______________
- ❑ Open year 'round ___Y___N

  dates__________________
- ❑ Check in time ___________
- ❑ Check out time __________
- ❑ Dog friendly ______Y ______N
- ❑ Max RV length ___________
- ❑ Distance from home

  miles: __________________

  hours: __________________
- ❑ Address________________

  ____

  ____

Fees:

- ❑ Day Use $ ___________
- ❑ Camp Sites $ _________
- ❑ RV Sites $ ___________
- ❑ Refund policy

  ____

  ____

  ____

Notes:

____

____

____

____

____

____

____

____

Make It Personal

Trip dates: | The weather was:

Why I went:

How I got there: (circle all that apply)

I went with:

We stayed in (space, cabin # etc):

Most relaxing day:

Something funny:

Someone we met:

Best story told:

We liked this:

The best food:

Games played:

Something disappointing:

Next time I'll do this differently:

Stephen F. Austin State Park

State: Texas   City: San Felipe   County: Austin

Plan your trip: https://tpwd.texas.gov/state-parks/stephen-f-austin

Activities:

- ❑ Archery
- ❑ Biking
- ❑ Boating
- ❑ Campfire
- ❑ Caving
- ❑ Disc Golf
- ❑ Fishing
- ❑ Geo Cache
- ❑ Golf
- ❑ Hiking
- ❑ Horseback
- ❑ Hunting
- ❑ Jr. Ranger
- ❑ Park Tours
- ❑ Rock Climbing
- ❑ Stargazing
- ❑ Swimming
- ❑ Wildlife & Birding
- ❑
- ❑

Facilities:

- ❑ ADA
- ❑ Gym
- ❑ Historic Sites
- ❑ Lodge
- ❑ Meeting hall
- ❑ Pavilions
- ❑ Picnic sites
- ❑ Pool
- ❑ Restrooms
- ❑ Showers
- ❑ Visitor center
- ❑ RV Camp
- ❑ Tent Camp
- ❑ Yurt Camp
- ❑ Cabins
- ❑ Lodge rooms
- ❑ Group barracks
- ❑ Screened shelter

Notes:

____

____

____

____

____

____

____

____

Get the Facts

- ❑ Phone (979) 885-3613
- ❑ Park Hours

____

- ❑ Reservations? _____Y _____N

date made_______________

- ❑ Open year 'round ___Y___N

dates_____________________

- ❑ Check in time ____________
- ❑ Check out time __________
- ❑ Dog friendly _____Y _____N
- ❑ Max RV length __________
- ❑ Distance from home

miles: ________________

hours: ________________

- ❑ Address________________

____

____

Fees:

- ❑ Day Use $ ___________
- ❑ Camp Sites $ _________
- ❑ RV Sites $ ___________
- ❑ Refund policy

____

____

____

Make It Personal

Trip dates: | The weather was:

Why I went:

How I got there: (circle all that apply)

I went with:

We stayed in (space, cabin # etc):

Most relaxing day:

Something funny:

Someone we met:

Best story told:

We liked this:

The best food:

Games played:

Something disappointing:

Next time I'll do this differently:

Tyler State Park
State: Texas   City: Tyler   County: Smith

Plan your trip: https://tpwd.texas.gov/state-parks/tyler

Activities:

- ❑ Archery
- ❑ Biking
- ❑ Boating
- ❑ Campfire
- ❑ Caving
- ❑ Disc Golf
- ❑ Fishing
- ❑ Geo Cache
- ❑ Golf
- ❑ Hiking
- ❑ Horseback
- ❑ Hunting
- ❑ Jr. Ranger
- ❑ Park Tours
- ❑ Rock Climbing
- ❑ Stargazing
- ❑ Swimming
- ❑ Wildlife & Birding
- ❑
- ❑

Facilities:

- ❑ ADA
- ❑ Gym
- ❑ Historic Sites
- ❑ Lodge
- ❑ Meeting hall
- ❑ Pavilions
- ❑ Picnic sites
- ❑ Pool
- ❑ Restrooms
- ❑ Showers
- ❑ Visitor center
- ❑ RV Camp
- ❑ Tent Camp
- ❑ Yurt Camp
- ❑ Cabins
- ❑ Lodge rooms
- ❑ Group barracks
- ❑ Screened shelter

Notes:

____

____

____

____

____

____

____

____

Get the Facts

- ❑ Phone (903) 597-5338
- ❑ Park Hours

  ____

- ❑ Reservations? ____Y ____N

  date made_______________

- ❑ Open year 'round ___Y___N

  dates__________________

- ❑ Check in time ___________
- ❑ Check out time __________
- ❑ Dog friendly _____Y _____N
- ❑ Max RV length __________
- ❑ Distance from home

  miles: ________________

  hours: ________________

- ❑ Address_______________

  ____

  ____

Fees:

- ❑ Day Use $ __________
- ❑ Camp Sites $ ________
- ❑ RV Sites $ __________
- ❑ Refund policy

  ____

  ____

Make It Personal

Trip dates:

The weather was:

Why I went:

How I got there: (circle all that apply)

I went with:

We stayed in (space, cabin # etc):

Most relaxing day:

Something funny:

Someone we met:

Best story told:

We liked this:

The best food:

Games played:

Something disappointing:

Next time I'll do this differently:

Village Creek State Park
State: Texas   City: Lumberton   County: Hardin

Plan your trip: https://tpwd.texas.gov/state-parks/village-creek

Activities:

- ❑ Archery
- ❑ Biking
- ❑ Boating
- ❑ Campfire
- ❑ Caving
- ❑ Disc Golf
- ❑ Fishing
- ❑ Geo Cache
- ❑ Golf
- ❑ Hiking
- ❑ Horseback
- ❑ Hunting
- ❑ Jr. Ranger
- ❑ Park Tours
- ❑ Rock Climbing
- ❑ Stargazing
- ❑ Swimming
- ❑ Wildlife & Birding
- ❑
- ❑

Facilities:

- ❑ ADA
- ❑ Gym
- ❑ Historic Sites
- ❑ Lodge
- ❑ Meeting hall
- ❑ Pavilions
- ❑ Picnic sites
- ❑ Pool
- ❑ Restrooms
- ❑ Showers
- ❑ Visitor center
- ❑ RV Camp
- ❑ Tent Camp
- ❑ Yurt Camp
- ❑ Cabins
- ❑ Lodge rooms
- ❑ Group barracks
- ❑ Screened shelter

Notes:

____

____

____

____

____

____

____

____

____

Get the Facts

- ❑ Phone (409) 755-7322
- ❑ Park Hours

____

- ❑ Reservations? _____Y _____N

date made_______________

- ❑ Open year 'round ___Y___N

dates__________________

- ❑ Check in time ___________
- ❑ Check out time __________
- ❑ Dog friendly _____Y _____N
- ❑ Max RV length __________
- ❑ Distance from home

miles: ________________

hours: ________________

- ❑ Address________________

____

____

Fees:

- ❑ Day Use $ ___________
- ❑ Camp Sites $ _________
- ❑ RV Sites $ ___________
- ❑ Refund policy

____

____

____

Make It Personal

Trip dates: The weather was:

Why I went:

How I got there: (circle all that apply)

I went with:

We stayed in (space, cabin # etc):

Most relaxing day:

Something funny:

Someone we met:

Best story told:

We liked this:

The best food:

Games played:

Something disappointing:

Next time I'll do this differently:

Barton Warnock Visitor Center

State: Texas　　　**City: Terlingua**　　　**County: Howard**

Plan your trip: https://tpwd.texas.gov/state-parks/barton-warnock

Activities:

- ❑ Bats
- ❑ Birding
- ❑ Guided tours
- ❑ Hiking
- ❑ Jr. Ranger
- ❑ Site Tours
- ❑ Wildlife
- ❑ -
- ❑ -
- ❑ -

Facilities:

- ❑ ADA
- ❑ Historic Sites
- ❑ Lodge
- ❑ Meeting hall
- ❑ Pavilions
- ❑ Picnic sites
- ❑ Restrooms
- ❑ Screened shelter
- ❑ Visitor center

Get the Facts

- ❑ Phone (432) 424-3327
- ❑ Park Hours

  ____

- ❑ Reservations? _____Y _____N

  date made_______________

- ❑ Open year 'round ___Y___N

  dates__________________

- ❑ Dog friendly _____Y _____N

- ❑ Distance from home

  miles: ________________

  hours: ________________

- ❑ Address________________

  ____

  ____

Wildlife Sited:

- ❑ -
- ❑ -
- ❑ -
- ❑ -
- ❑ -

- ❑ -
- ❑ -
- ❑ -
- ❑ -
- ❑ -

Notes:

____

____

____

____

____

____

____

____

____

Fees:

- ❑ Day Use $ ___________
- ❑ Refund policy

  ____

  ____

  ____

Notes: At the eastern entrance for Big Bend Ranch State Park

Battleship Texas State Historic Site

State: Texas   City: LaPorte   County: Harris

Plan your trip: https://tpwd.texas.gov/state-parks/battleship-texas

Activities:

- ❑ Bats
- ❑ Birding
- ❑ Guided tours
- ❑ Hiking
- ❑ Jr. Ranger
- ❑ Site Tours
- ❑ Wildlife
- ❑ -
- ❑ -
- ❑ -

Wildlife Sited:

- ❑ -
- ❑ -
- ❑ -
- ❑ -
- ❑ -

- ❑ -
- ❑ -
- ❑ -
- ❑ -
- ❑ -

Facilities:

- ❑ ADA
- ❑ Historic Sites
- ❑ Lodge
- ❑ Meeting hall
- ❑ Pavilions
- ❑ Picnic sites
- ❑ Restrooms
- ❑ Screened shelter
- ❑ Visitor center

Get the Facts

- ❑ Phone (281) 479-2431
- ❑ Park Hours

____

- ❑ Reservations? ____Y ____N

date made_______________

- ❑ Open year 'round ___Y___N

dates___________________

- ❑ Dog friendly _____Y _____N
- ❑ Distance from home

miles: _________________

hours: _________________

- ❑ Address_______________

____

____

Notes:

____

____

____

____

____

____

____

____

Fees:

- ❑ Day Use $ ___________
- ❑ Refund policy

____

____

____

Notes:

Devil's Sinkhole State Natural Area

State: Texas   City: Rocksprings   County: Edwards

Plan your trip: https://tpwd.texas.gov/state-parks/devils-sinkhole

Activities:

- ❑ Bats
- ❑ Birding
- ❑ Guided tours
- ❑ Hiking
- ❑ Jr. Ranger
- ❑ Site Tours
- ❑ Wildlife
- ❑ -
- ❑ -
- ❑ -

Facilities:

- ❑ ADA
- ❑ Historic Sites
- ❑ Lodge
- ❑ Meeting hall
- ❑ Pavilions
- ❑ Picnic sites
- ❑ Restrooms
- ❑ Screened shelter
- ❑ Visitor center

Get the Facts

- ❑ Phone (830) 683-2287
- ❑ Park Hours

  ____

- ❑ Reservations? _____Y _____N

  date made_______________

- ❑ Open year 'round ___Y___N

  dates__________________

- ❑ Dog friendly _____Y _____N

- ❑ Distance from home

  miles: _______________

  hours: _______________

- ❑ Address_______________

  ____

  ____

Wildlife Sited:

- ❑ -
- ❑ -
- ❑ -
- ❑ -
- ❑ -

- ❑ -
- ❑ -
- ❑ -
- ❑ -
- ❑ -

Fees:

- ❑ Day Use $ _____________
- ❑ Refund policy

  ____

  ____

  ____

Notes:

____

____

____

____

____

____

____

____

____

Notes: Access is only by guided tour. Nearby: Kickapoo Cavern State Park

Fort Leaton State Historic Site

State: Texas   City: Presidio   County: Presidio

Plan your trip: https://tpwd.texas.gov/state-parks/fort-leaton

Activities:

- ❑ Bats
- ❑ Birding
- ❑ Guided tours
- ❑ Hiking
- ❑ Jr. Ranger
- ❑ Site Tours
- ❑ Wildlife
- ❑ -
- ❑ -
- ❑ -

Facilities:

- ❑ ADA
- ❑ Historic Sites
- ❑ Lodge
- ❑ Meeting hall
- ❑ Pavilions
- ❑ Picnic sites
- ❑ Restrooms
- ❑ Screened shelter
- ❑ Visitor center

Get the Facts

- ❑ Phone (432) 229-3613
- ❑ Park Hours

  ____

- ❑ Reservations? ____Y ____N

  date made______________

- ❑ Open year 'round ___Y___N

  dates__________________

- ❑ Dog friendly ______Y ______N

- ❑ Distance from home

  miles: ________________

  hours: ________________

- ❑ Address________________

  ____

  ____

Wildlife Sited:

- ❑ -
- ❑ -
- ❑ -
- ❑ -
- ❑ -

- ❑ -
- ❑ -
- ❑ -
- ❑ -
- ❑ -

Notes:

____
____
____
____
____
____
____
____
____

Fees:

- ❑ Day Use $ ___________
- ❑ Refund policy

  ____

  ____

  ____

Notes: Located at the western entrance to Big Bend Ranch State Park

Goliad Area Historic Sites

State: Texas   **City: Goliad**   **County: Goliad**

Plan your trip: https://tpwd.texas.gov/state-parks/goliad/goliad-area-historic-sites#rosario

Activities:

- ❑ Guided tours
- ❑ Hiking
- ❑ Jr. Ranger
- ❑ Site Tours
- ❑ Wildlife
- ❑ Museum

Facilities:

- ❑ ADA
- ❑ Historic Sites
- ❑ Restrooms
- ❑ Screened shelter
- ❑ Visitor center
- ❑

Get the Facts

- ❑ Phone (361) 645-3405
- ❑ Park Hours

  ____

- ❑ Reservations? _____Y _____N

  date made______________

- ❑ Open year 'round ___Y___N

  dates__________________

- ❑ Dog friendly ______Y ______N

- ❑ Distance from home

  miles: ________________

  hours: ________________

- ❑ Address________________

  ____

  ____

Area Attractions:

- ❑ Mission Espíritu Santo State Historic Site
- ❑ El Camino Real de los Tejas Visitors Center
- ❑ Zaragoza Birthplace State Historic Site
- ❑ Mission Rosario State Historic Site
- ❑ Presidio La Bahía
- ❑ Fannin Memorial Monument
- ❑ Angel of Goliad Nature Trail & Plaza

Notes

____

____

____

____

____

____

____

____

____

Fees:

- ❑ Day Use $ ____________
- ❑ Refund policy

  ____

  ____

  ____

Notes: The Town of Goliad has many historical sites and battlefields to visit.

Honey Creek State Natural Area
State: Texas   City: Spring Branch   County: Comal

Plan your trip: https://tpwd.texas.gov/state-parks/honey-creek

Activities:

- ❏ Bats
- ❏ Birding
- ❏ Guided tours
- ❏ Hiking
- ❏ Jr. Ranger
- ❏ Site Tours
- ❏ Wildlife
- ❏ -
- ❏ -
- ❏ -

Wildlife Sited:

- ❏ -
- ❏ -
- ❏ -
- ❏ -
- ❏ -

- ❏ -
- ❏ -
- ❏ -
- ❏ -
- ❏ -

Notes:

____
____
____
____
____
____
____
____
____
____

Facilities:

- ❏ ADA
- ❏ Historic Sites
- ❏ Lodge
- ❏ Meeting hall
- ❏ Pavilions
- ❏ Picnic sites
- ❏ Restrooms
- ❏ Screened shelter
- ❏ Visitor center

Get the Facts

- ❏ Phone (830) 438-2656
- ❏ Park Hours

  ____

- ❏ Reservations? ____Y ____N

  date made______________

- ❏ Open year 'round ___Y___N

  dates__________________

- ❏ Dog friendly ______Y ______N

- ❏ Distance from home

  miles: ________________

  hours: ________________

- ❏ Address________________

  ____

  ____

Fees:

- ❏ Day Use $ ___________
- ❏ Refund policy

  ____

  ____

  ____

Notes: Entry is by guided tours only. Adjacent to Guadalupe River State Park.

Longhorn Cavern State Park

State: Texas   **City: Burnet**   **County: Burnet**

Plan your trip: https://tpwd.texas.gov/state-parks/longhorn-cavern

Activities:

- ❑ Bats
- ❑ Birding
- ❑ Guided tours
- ❑ Hiking
- ❑ Jr. Ranger
- ❑ Site Tours
- ❑ Wildlife
- ❑ -
- ❑ -
- ❑ -

Facilities:

- ❑ ADA
- ❑ Historic Sites
- ❑ Restrooms
- ❑ Screened shelter
- ❑ Visitor center
- ❑ -
- ❑ -
- ❑ -
- ❑ -
- ❑ -

Get the Facts

- ❑ Phone (512) 715-9000
- ❑ Park Hours

  ____

- ❑ Reservations? _____Y _____N

  date made_______________
- ❑ Open year 'round ___Y___N

  dates__________________
- ❑ Dog friendly _____Y _____N
- ❑ Distance from home

  miles: ________________

  hours: ________________
- ❑ Address_______________

  ____

  ____

Wildlife Sited:

- ❑ -
- ❑ -
- ❑ -
- ❑ -
- ❑ -

- ❑ -
- ❑ -
- ❑ -
- ❑ -
- ❑ -

Fees:

- ❑ Day Use $ ___________
- ❑ Refund policy

  ____

  ____

  ____

Notes:

____

____

____

____

____

____

____

____

Notes: Camping nearby at Inks Lake State Park

Lyndon B. Johnson State Park & Historic Site

State: Texas   City: Stonewall   County: Gillespie

Plan your trip: https://tpwd.texas.gov/state-parks/lyndon-b-johnson

Activities:

- ❑ Bats
- ❑ Birding
- ❑ Guided tours
- ❑ Hiking
- ❑ Jr. Ranger
- ❑ Site Tours
- ❑ Wildlife
- ❑ -
- ❑ -
- ❑ -

Facilities:

- ❑ ADA
- ❑ Historic Sites
- ❑ Restrooms
- ❑ Screened shelter
- ❑ Visitor center
- ❑ Swimming pool
- ❑ Tennis courts
- ❑ -
- ❑ -
- ❑ -

Get the Facts

- ❑ Phone (830) 644-2252
- ❑ Park Hours

  ____

- ❑ Reservations? ____Y ____N

  date made____________

- ❑ Open year 'round ___Y___N

  dates________________

- ❑ Dog friendly _____Y _____N

- ❑ Distance from home

  miles: ________________

  hours: ________________

- ❑ Address________________

  ____

  ____

Wildlife Sited:

- ❑ -
- ❑ -
- ❑ -
- ❑ -
- ❑ -

- ❑ -
- ❑ -
- ❑ -
- ❑ -
- ❑ -

Notes:

____

____

____

____

____

____

____

____

____

Fees:

- ❑ Day Use $ ___________
- ❑ Refund policy

  ____

  ____

  ____

Notes: Within walking distance = Sauer-Beckman Living History Farm, Behrens Cabins, and LBJ Ranch.

Old Tunnel State Park
State: Texas   City: Fredericksburg   County: Gillespie

Plan your trip: https://tpwd.texas.gov/state-parks/old-tunnel

Activities:

- ❑ Bats
- ❑ Birding
- ❑ Guided tours
- ❑ Hiking
- ❑ Jr. Ranger
- ❑ Site Tours
- ❑ Wildlife
- ❑ -
- ❑ -
- ❑ -

Facilities:

- ❑ ADA
- ❑ Historic Sites
- ❑ Restrooms
- ❑ Screened shelter
- ❑ Visitor center
- ❑ Swimming pool
- ❑ Tennis courts
- ❑ -
- ❑ -
- ❑ -

Get the Facts

- ❑ Phone (866) 978-2287
- ❑ Park Hours

  ____

- ❑ Reservations? _____Y _____N

  date made_______________

- ❑ Open year 'round ___Y___N

  dates__________________

- ❑ Dog friendly _____Y _____N

- ❑ Distance from home

  miles: _______________

  hours: _______________

- ❑ Address_______________

  ____

  ____

Wildlife Sited:

- ❑ -
- ❑ -
- ❑ -
- ❑ -
- ❑ -

- ❑ -
- ❑ -
- ❑ -
- ❑ -
- ❑ -

Fees:

- ❑ Day Use $ ___________
- ❑ Refund policy

  ____

  ____

  ____

Notes:

____

____

____

____

____

____

____

____

Notes:

Resaca de la Palma State Park

State: Texas   City: Brownsville   County: Cameron

Plan your trip: https://tpwd.texas.gov/state-parks/resaca-de-la-palma

Activities:

- ❑ Bats
- ❑ Birding
- ❑ Guided tours
- ❑ Hiking
- ❑ Jr. Ranger
- ❑ Self Tours
- ❑ Wildlife
- ❑ -
- ❑ -
- ❑ -

Wildlife Sited:

- ❑ -
- ❑ -
- ❑ -
- ❑ -
- ❑ -

- ❑ -
- ❑ -
- ❑ -
- ❑ -
- ❑ -

Facilities:

- ❑ ADA
- ❑ Historic Sites
- ❑ Restrooms
- ❑ Screened shelter
- ❑ Visitor center
- ❑ -
- ❑ -
- ❑ -
- ❑ -
- ❑ -

Get the Facts

- ❑ Phone (956) 350-2920
- ❑ Park Hours

  ____

- ❑ Reservations? ____Y ____N

  date made_______________
- ❑ Open year 'round ___Y___N

  dates_________________
- ❑ Dog friendly ______Y ______N
- ❑ Distance from home

  miles: _______________

  hours: _______________
- ❑ Address_________________

  ____

  ____

Fees:

- ❑ Day Use $ __________
- ❑ Refund policy

  ____

  ____

  ____

Notes:

____

____

____

____

____

____

____

____

Notes:

Sheldon Lake State Park & Environmental Learning Center

State: Texas   City: Houston   County: Harris

Plan your trip: https://tpwd.texas.gov/state-parks/sheldon-lake

Activities:

- ❑ Bats
- ❑ Birding
- ❑ Guided tours
- ❑ Hiking
- ❑ Jr. Ranger
- ❑ Self Tours
- ❑ Wildlife
- ❑ Fishing
- ❑ -
- ❑ -

Facilities:

- ❑ ADA
- ❑ Historic Sites
- ❑ Restrooms
- ❑ Screened shelter
- ❑ Visitor center
- ❑ -
- ❑ -
- ❑ -
- ❑ -
- ❑ -

Get the Facts

- ❑ Phone (281) 456-2800
- ❑ Park Hours
  ____
- ❑ Reservations? ____Y ____N
  date made______________
- ❑ Open year 'round ___Y___N
  dates__________________
- ❑ Dog friendly _____Y _____N
- ❑ Distance from home
  miles: ________________
  hours: ________________
- ❑ Address________________
  ____
  ____

Wildlife Sited:

- ❑ -
- ❑ -
- ❑ -
- ❑ -
- ❑ -

- ❑ -
- ❑ -
- ❑ -
- ❑ -
- ❑ -

Fees:

- ❑ Day Use $ ___________
- ❑ Refund policy
  ____
  ____
  ____

Notes:

____
____
____
____
____
____
____
____

Notes:

Wyler Aerial Tramway

State: Texas   City: El Paso   County: El Paso

Plan your trip: https://tpwd.texas.gov/state-parks/wyler-aerial-tramway

Activities:

- ❑ Bats
- ❑ Birding
- ❑ Guided tours
- ❑ Hiking
- ❑ Jr. Ranger
- ❑ Self Tours
- ❑ Wildlife
- ❑ Fishing
- ❑ -
- ❑ -

Facilities:

- ❑ ADA
- ❑ Historic Sites
- ❑ Restrooms
- ❑ Screened shelter
- ❑ Visitor center
- ❑ -
- ❑ -
- ❑ -
- ❑ -
- ❑ -

Get the Facts

- ❑ Phone (915) 566-6622
- ❑ Park Hours

  ____

- ❑ Reservations? _____Y _____N

  date made_______________

- ❑ Open year 'round ___Y___N

  dates___________________

- ❑ Dog friendly _____Y _____N
- ❑ Distance from home

  miles: _________________

  hours: _________________

- ❑ Address_______________

  ____

  ____

Wildlife Sited:

- ❑ -
- ❑ -
- ❑ -
- ❑ -
- ❑ -

- ❑ -
- ❑ -
- ❑ -
- ❑ -
- ❑ -

Fees:

- ❑ Day Use $ ___________
- ❑ Refund policy

  ____

  ____

  ____

Notes: Located at Franklin Mountains State Park

Notes:

____

____

____

____

____

____

____

____

Name:

State: Texas   **City:**   **County:**

Plan your trip:

- ❑ Archery
- ❑ Biking
- ❑ Boating
- ❑ Campfire
- ❑ Caving
- ❑ Disc Golf
- ❑ Fishing
- ❑ Geo Cache
- ❑ Golf
- ❑ Hiking
- ❑ Horseback
- ❑ Hunting
- ❑ Jr. Ranger
- ❑ Park Tours
- ❑ Rock Climbing
- ❑ Stargazing
- ❑ Swimming
- ❑ Wildlife & Birding
- ❑
- ❑

- ❑ ADA
- ❑ Gym
- ❑ Historic Sites
- ❑ Lodge
- ❑ Meeting hall
- ❑ Pavilions
- ❑ Picnic sites
- ❑ Pool
- ❑ Restrooms
- ❑ Showers
- ❑ Visitor center
- ❑ RV Camp
- ❑ Tent Camp
- ❑ Yurt Camp
- ❑ Cabins
- ❑ Lodge rooms
- ❑ Group barracks
- ❑ Screened shelter

____
____
____
____
____
____
____

- ❑ Phone
- ❑ Park Hours

____

- ❑ Reservations? _____Y _____N

date made_______________

- ❑ Open year 'round ___Y___N

dates___________________

- ❑ Check in time ___________
- ❑ Check out time __________
- ❑ Dog friendly ______Y ______N
- ❑ Max RV length __________
- ❑ Distance from home

miles: _________________

hours: _________________

- ❑ Address_________________

____

- ❑ Day Use $ ___________
- ❑ Camp Sites $ _________
- ❑ RV Sites $ __________
- ❑ Refund policy

____
____
____

Make It Personal

Trip dates: | The weather was:

Why I went:

How I got there: (circle all that apply)

I went with:

We stayed in (space, cabin # etc):

Most relaxing day:

Something funny:

Someone we met:

Best story told:

We liked this:

The best food:

Games played:

Something disappointing:

Next time I'll do this differently:

Name:

State: Texas **City:** **County:**

Plan your trip:

- ❑ Archery
- ❑ Biking
- ❑ Boating
- ❑ Campfire
- ❑ Caving
- ❑ Disc Golf
- ❑ Fishing
- ❑ Geo Cache
- ❑ Golf
- ❑ Hiking
- ❑ Horseback
- ❑ Hunting
- ❑ Jr. Ranger
- ❑ Park Tours
- ❑ Rock Climbing
- ❑ Stargazing
- ❑ Swimming
- ❑ Wildlife & Birding
- ❑
- ❑

- ❑ ADA
- ❑ Gym
- ❑ Historic Sites
- ❑ Lodge
- ❑ Meeting hall
- ❑ Pavilions
- ❑ Picnic sites
- ❑ Pool
- ❑ Restrooms
- ❑ Showers
- ❑ Visitor center
- ❑ RV Camp
- ❑ Tent Camp
- ❑ Yurt Camp
- ❑ Cabins
- ❑ Lodge rooms
- ❑ Group barracks
- ❑ Screened shelter

____

____

____

____

____

____

____

____

- ❑ Phone
- ❑ Park Hours

____

- ❑ Reservations? ____Y ____N

  date made________________

- ❑ Open year 'round ___Y___N

  dates___________________

- ❑ Check in time ___________

- ❑ Check out time __________

- ❑ Dog friendly _____Y _____N

- ❑ Max RV length __________

- ❑ Distance from home

  miles: ________________

  hours: ________________

- ❑ Address________________

____

____

- ❑ Day Use $ __________
- ❑ Camp Sites $ _________
- ❑ RV Sites $ __________
- ❑ Refund policy

____

____

____

Make It Personal

Trip dates: ___________________ | The weather was:

Why I went: ___________________

How I got there: (circle all that apply)

I went with: ___________________

We stayed in (space, cabin # etc): ___________________

Most relaxing day: ___________________

Something funny: ___________________

Someone we met: ___________________

Best story told: ___________________

We liked this: ___________________

The best food: ___________________

Games played: ___________________

Something disappointing: ___________________

Next time I'll do this differently: ___________________

Name:
State: Texas   **City:**   **County:**

Plan your trip:

Activities:

- ❏ Archery
- ❏ Biking
- ❏ Boating
- ❏ Campfire
- ❏ Caving
- ❏ Disc Golf
- ❏ Fishing
- ❏ Geo Cache
- ❏ Golf
- ❏ Hiking
- ❏ Horseback
- ❏ Hunting
- ❏ Jr. Ranger
- ❏ Park Tours
- ❏ Rock Climbing
- ❏ Stargazing
- ❏ Swimming
- ❏ Wildlife & Birding
- ❏
- ❏

Facilities:

- ❏ ADA
- ❏ Gym
- ❏ Historic Sites
- ❏ Lodge
- ❏ Meeting hall
- ❏ Pavilions
- ❏ Picnic sites
- ❏ Pool
- ❏ Restrooms
- ❏ Showers
- ❏ Visitor center
- ❏ RV Camp
- ❏ Tent Camp
- ❏ Yurt Camp
- ❏ Cabins
- ❏ Lodge rooms
- ❏ Group barracks
- ❏ Screened shelter

Notes:

____

____

____

____

____

____

____

____

Get the Facts

- ❏ Phone
- ❏ Park Hours

____

- ❏ Reservations? ____Y ____N

date made________________

- ❏ Open year 'round ___Y___N

dates____________________

- ❏ Check in time ___________
- ❏ Check out time __________
- ❏ Dog friendly _____Y _____N
- ❏ Max RV length __________
- ❏ Distance from home

miles: __________________

hours: __________________

- ❏ Address________________

____

____

Fees:

- ❏ Day Use $ ___________
- ❏ Camp Sites $ _________
- ❏ RV Sites $ ___________
- ❏ Refund policy

____

____

____

Make It Personal

Trip dates:

The weather was:

Why I went:

How I got there: (circle all that apply)

I went with:

We stayed in (space, cabin # etc):

Most relaxing day:

Something funny:

Someone we met:

Best story told:

We liked this:

The best food:

Games played:

Something disappointing:

Next time I'll do this differently:

Name:

State: Texas   **City:**   **County:**

Plan your trip:

Activities:

- ❑ Archery
- ❑ Biking
- ❑ Boating
- ❑ Campfire
- ❑ Caving
- ❑ Disc Golf
- ❑ Fishing
- ❑ Geo Cache
- ❑ Golf
- ❑ Hiking
- ❑ Horseback
- ❑ Hunting
- ❑ Jr. Ranger
- ❑ Park Tours
- ❑ Rock Climbing
- ❑ Stargazing
- ❑ Swimming
- ❑ Wildlife & Birding
- ❑
- ❑

Facilities:

- ❑ ADA
- ❑ Gym
- ❑ Historic Sites
- ❑ Lodge
- ❑ Meeting hall
- ❑ Pavilions
- ❑ Picnic sites
- ❑ Pool
- ❑ Restrooms
- ❑ Showers
- ❑ Visitor center
- ❑ RV Camp
- ❑ Tent Camp
- ❑ Yurt Camp
- ❑ Cabins
- ❑ Lodge rooms
- ❑ Group barracks
- ❑ Screened shelter

Notes:

____

____

____

____

____

____

____

____

____

Get the Facts

- ❑ Phone
- ❑ Park Hours

____

- ❑ Reservations? _____Y _____N

date made________________

- ❑ Open year 'round ___Y___N

dates__________________

- ❑ Check in time ____________
- ❑ Check out time ___________
- ❑ Dog friendly ______Y _____N
- ❑ Max RV length ___________
- ❑ Distance from home

miles: __________________

hours: __________________

- ❑ Address__________________

____

____

Fees:

- ❑ Day Use $ ____________
- ❑ Camp Sites $ _________
- ❑ RV Sites $ ___________
- ❑ Refund policy

____

____

Make It Personal

Trip dates: ___________________ | The weather was:

Why I went:
____

How I got there: (circle all that apply)

I went with:
____

We stayed in (space, cabin # etc):
____

Most relaxing day:
____

Something funny:
____

Someone we met:
____

Best story told:
____

We liked this:
____

The best food:
____

Games played:
____

Something disappointing:
____

Next time I'll do this differently:
____

Name:

State: Texas   City: County:

Plan your trip:

Activities:

- ❑ Archery
- ❑ Biking
- ❑ Boating
- ❑ Campfire
- ❑ Caving
- ❑ Disc Golf
- ❑ Fishing
- ❑ Geo Cache
- ❑ Golf
- ❑ Hiking
- ❑ Horseback
- ❑ Hunting
- ❑ Jr. Ranger
- ❑ Park Tours
- ❑ Rock Climbing
- ❑ Stargazing
- ❑ Swimming
- ❑ Wildlife & Birding
- ❑
- ❑

Facilities:

- ❑ ADA
- ❑ Gym
- ❑ Historic Sites
- ❑ Lodge
- ❑ Meeting hall
- ❑ Pavilions
- ❑ Picnic sites
- ❑ Pool
- ❑ Restrooms
- ❑ Showers
- ❑ Visitor center
- ❑ RV Camp
- ❑ Tent Camp
- ❑ Yurt Camp
- ❑ Cabins
- ❑ Lodge rooms
- ❑ Group barracks
- ❑ Screened shelter

Get the Facts

- ❑ Phone
- ❑ Park Hours

____

- ❑ Reservations? ____Y ____N

date made_______________

- ❑ Open year 'round ___Y___N

dates__________________

- ❑ Check in time ___________
- ❑ Check out time __________
- ❑ Dog friendly _____Y _____N
- ❑ Max RV length _________
- ❑ Distance from home

miles: ________________

hours: ________________

- ❑ Address______________

____

____

Fees:

- ❑ Day Use $ __________
- ❑ Camp Sites $ ________
- ❑ RV Sites $ __________
- ❑ Refund policy

____

____

____

Notes:

____

____

____

____

____

____

____

____

____

Make It Personal

Trip dates: | The weather was:

Why I went:

How I got there: (circle all that apply)

I went with:

We stayed in (space, cabin # etc):

Most relaxing day:

Something funny:

Someone we met:

Best story told:

We liked this:

The best food:

Games played:

Something disappointing:

Next time I'll do this differently:

Name:

State: Texas   **City:**   **County:**

Plan your trip:

Activities:

- ❑ Bats
- ❑ Birding
- ❑ Guided tours
- ❑ Hiking
- ❑ Jr. Ranger
- ❑ Site Tours
- ❑ Wildlife
- ❑ -
- ❑ -
- ❑ -

Wildlife Sited:

- ❑ -
- ❑ -
- ❑ -
- ❑ -
- ❑ -

- ❑ -
- ❑ -
- ❑ -
- ❑ -
- ❑ -

Notes:

Facilities:

- ❑ ADA
- ❑ Historic Sites
- ❑ Lodge
- ❑ Meeting hall
- ❑ Pavilions
- ❑ Picnic sites
- ❑ Restrooms
- ❑ Screened shelter
- ❑ Visitor center

Get the Facts

- ❑ Phone
- ❑ Park Hours

  ____

- ❑ Reservations? ____Y ____N

  date made______________
- ❑ Open year 'round ___Y___N

  dates______________
- ❑ Dog friendly _____Y _____N
- ❑ Distance from home

  miles: ______________

  hours: ______________
- ❑ Address______________

  ____

  ____

Fees:

- ❑ Day Use $ ____________
- ❑ Refund policy

  ____

  ____

  ____

Notes:.

Name:

State: Texas **City:** **County:**

Plan your trip:

Activities:

- ❑ Bats
- ❑ Birding
- ❑ Guided tours
- ❑ Hiking
- ❑ Jr. Ranger
- ❑ Site Tours
- ❑ Wildlife
- ❑ -
- ❑ -
- ❑ -

Wildlife Sited:

- ❑ -
- ❑ -
- ❑ -
- ❑ -
- ❑ -

- ❑ -
- ❑ -
- ❑ -
- ❑ -
- ❑ -

Facilities:

- ❑ ADA
- ❑ Historic Sites
- ❑ Lodge
- ❑ Meeting hall
- ❑ Pavilions
- ❑ Picnic sites
- ❑ Restrooms
- ❑ Screened shelter
- ❑ Visitor center

Get the Facts

- ❑ Phone
- ❑ Park Hours

____

- ❑ Reservations? ____Y ____N

  date made_____________
- ❑ Open year 'round ___Y___N

  dates________________
- ❑ Dog friendly _____Y _____N
- ❑ Distance from home

  miles: _______________

  hours: _______________
- ❑ Address______________

  ____

  ____

Fees:

- ❑ Day Use $ ___________
- ❑ Refund policy

  ____

  ____

  ____

Notes:.

Notes:

Name:

State: Texas   City: County:

Plan your trip:

Activities:

- ❑ Bats
- ❑ Birding
- ❑ Guided tours
- ❑ Hiking
- ❑ Jr. Ranger
- ❑ Site Tours
- ❑ Wildlife
- ❑ -
- ❑ -
- ❑ -

Facilities:

- ❑ ADA
- ❑ Historic Sites
- ❑ Lodge
- ❑ Meeting hall
- ❑ Pavilions
- ❑ Picnic sites
- ❑ Restrooms
- ❑ Screened shelter
- ❑ Visitor center

Get the Facts

- ❑ Phone
- ❑ Park Hours

  ____

- ❑ Reservations? ____Y ____N

  date made_______________

- ❑ Open year 'round ___Y___N

  dates_________________

- ❑ Dog friendly _____Y _____N
- ❑ Distance from home

  miles: ________________

  hours: ________________

- ❑ Address________________

  ____

  ____

Wildlife Sited:

- ❑ -
- ❑ -
- ❑ -
- ❑ -
- ❑ -

- ❑ -
- ❑ -
- ❑ -
- ❑ -
- ❑ -

Fees:

- ❑ Day Use $ __________
- ❑ Refund policy

  ____

  ____

  ____

Notes:

____

____

____

____

____

____

____

____

____

Notes:.

Name:

State: Texas   City: County:

Plan your trip:

Activities:

- ❏ Bats
- ❏ Birding
- ❏ Guided tours
- ❏ Hiking
- ❏ Jr. Ranger
- ❏ Site Tours
- ❏ Wildlife
- ❏ -
- ❏ -
- ❏ -

Facilities:

- ❏ ADA
- ❏ Historic Sites
- ❏ Lodge
- ❏ Meeting hall
- ❏ Pavilions
- ❏ Picnic sites
- ❏ Restrooms
- ❏ Screened shelter
- ❏ Visitor center

Get the Facts

- ❏ Phone
- ❏ Park Hours

  ____

- ❏ Reservations? ____Y ____N

  date made______________

- ❏ Open year 'round ___Y___N

  dates__________________

- ❏ Dog friendly _____Y _____N

- ❏ Distance from home

  miles: ________________

  hours: ________________

- ❏ Address________________

  ____

  ____

Wildlife Sited:

- ❏ -
- ❏ -
- ❏ -
- ❏ -
- ❏ -

- ❏ -
- ❏ -
- ❏ -
- ❏ -
- ❏ -

Fees:

- ❏ Day Use $ ___________
- ❏ Refund policy

  ____

  ____

  ____

Notes:

____

____

____

____

____

____

____

____

Notes:.

Name:

State: Texas　　　City:　　　County:

Plan your trip:

- ❑ Bats
- ❑ Birding
- ❑ Guided tours
- ❑ Hiking
- ❑ Jr. Ranger
- ❑ Site Tours
- ❑ Wildlife
- ❑ -
- ❑ -
- ❑ -

- ❑ -
- ❑ -
- ❑ -
- ❑ -
- ❑ -

- ❑ -
- ❑ -
- ❑ -
- ❑ -
- ❑ -

____

____

____

____

____

____

____

____

- ❑ ADA
- ❑ Historic Sites
- ❑ Lodge
- ❑ Meeting hall
- ❑ Pavilions
- ❑ Picnic sites
- ❑ Restrooms
- ❑ Screened shelter
- ❑ Visitor center

- ❑ Phone
- ❑ Park Hours

____

- ❑ Reservations? ____Y ____N

date made________________

- ❑ Open year 'round ___Y___N

dates____________________

- ❑ Dog friendly _____Y _____N
- ❑ Distance from home

miles: ________________

hours: ________________

- ❑ Address________________

____

____

- ❑ Day Use $ ___________
- ❑ Refund policy

____

____

____